30 DAYS TO

CONCEALEDCARRY
CONFIDENCE

TomMcHale

Printed in the United States
ISBN 978-0-9967874-4-4
30 Days To Concealed Carry Confidence, Second Printing
Written by Tom McHale
Cover Designed by Dylan Hopf
Designed by Dusty Reid and Kelly Welke
Edited by Jason Braun, Carla Dickmann and Raven Moerchen

The information in this book is for informational purposes
only and does not constitute legal advice. For specific
questions, you should consult a qualified attorney.

If you're the kind of person who's reading this, that means you've already made the most important decision: You've decided that you — and you alone — are responsible for your own safety and the safety of your loved ones.

Though that's the most important decision, it certainly won't be the last you have to make. You're going to carry concealed, but if you don't already have a preferred pistol or revolver, which should you choose? If you've never carried a sidearm before, what kind of holster should you use to do so? If you've never bought defense-specific ammunition — or maybe never even bought ammunition of any kind — what kind of rounds should you carry? Is a loaded gun in a holster all you need?

The most common question Executive Editor Kevin Michalowski and I get about our everyday carry (EDC) gear is, "What do you carry?" A decent number of folks don't want to try anything out or do any research … they just want to know what we carry and then go buy it.

I understand how this happens. We do, after all, assess and review countless holsters, guns, flashlights and ammo. But what's perfect for us might not be even close to appropriate for someone else.

I'm fond of saying that what we do here at the United States Concealed Carry Association is get the right guns in the right hands. What this means to me and the rest of the staff at the USCCA is that you (as a responsibly armed American) need to get what works for you, be it revolver or semi-automatic, inside or outside the waistband, Kydex or leather or anything else.

Atop all of the equipment concerns, you'll have countless questions about lethal force decision-making, travel, how to navigate the sometimes tricky social considerations of the responsibly armed lifestyle and more. We here at the USCCA want to help you on your journey, and we humbly ask that you reach out to us if you ever have any questions about any aspect of concealed carry, self-defense or your own personal-security plan.

Stay alert, stay focused and stay safe,

Ed Combs
Associate Editor, *Concealed Carry Magazine*

CONTENTS

30 DAYS TO CONCEALED CARRY CONFIDENCE

You might be surprised at what you can accomplish in 30 days.

What if I told you that if you follow this program faithfully and do the at-home and range practice it recommends, you will have completed more focused skill development in 30 days than the vast majority of recreational shooters rack up in years? Put another way, if you put your mind to it, you will be able to go from novice to accomplished (and safe) gun owner at an astounding pace.

You will not be a self-defense expert at the end of this 30 days. Continuing study, training and practice will always be required. This program will not only get you started but will also equip you with the tools to build on what you learn here. Like any other skill, defensive shooting is a never-ending learning process. As long as you adopt an attitude of being a lifelong student, you'll have the mindset required to use a gun for self-defense. Think of home and self-defense as graduate-level classes that never end.

If you are considering using a gun for personal defense, there is a lot to learn. Learning how to safely operate a handgun is just the tip of the iceberg. Here's a preview of just some of the knowledge and skills you will need to acquire:

You will need to know if you're capable and ready to take a life if yours depends on it.

You will need to learn about the dangers of a false sense of security. Simply having a gun means nothing unless you have the tools and knowledge to make it work for you, not against you.

You will need to learn about concealed carry laws. When and where can you carry a gun?

You will need to learn about self-defense law. What defines legitimate self-defense, and what scenarios will put you behind bars?

You will need to understand when you can and cannot use a gun for self-defense. Can you shoot an unarmed attacker? What factors determine whether you can or can't?

You will need to understand that killing someone else is homicide, even when circumstances clearly point to a legitimate self-defense scenario. There are no free passes. Here, you will learn ways to minimize the impact of your worst legal nightmare.

You will need to know what a firearm can and, more importantly, can't do to help stop a determined attacker.

You will need to understand different types of firearms and how to evaluate their respective pros and cons for your specific situation.

You will need to think about how to store your gun at home to make sure it's useful in an emergency but secure the rest of the time.

You will need to decide how to carry a gun and how to evaluate real pros and cons of different carry methods. Which ones might be providing a false sense of security given your specific lifestyle?

You will need to think about carrying in the car on your way to or from work or school. You will also need to think about how you spend your days, along with limitations that may alter your concealed carry strategy.

You will need to learn how to shoot accurately under stress — not just at stationary targets on the range but also while you and your target are moving.

You will need to know how to draw and use your gun instinctively in a real-world scenario — not just in the artificial environment of a shooting range.

You will need to know how to communicate with your family and how to make workable plans in advance of a bad situation.

You will need to know how to make the most of your time at the shooting range and how you can gain tangible performance improvements right at home.

Most importantly, you will always need to be aware of the things you do not know. Using a gun as part of your overall self-defense strategy is a never-ending quest for advancing knowledge and skill. Here, we will help you learn ways to honestly assess areas that need improvement.

We are going to cover all these topics and more over the next 30 days. If you really want to make the most of your month-long investment, don't skimp on the homework. It's there for a reason. As a simple example, if you spend 10 minutes a day just practicing routine drills such as drawing from a holster, dry-firing and changing magazines, you'll be far more skilled at the end of one month than the vast majority of gun owners out there. Most of them go to the range and plink at targets once in a while. Here, you'll be using your time wisely to actually develop specific skills. Trust us on this one. You'll be amazed at the results you'll get from even a small time commitment to daily practice.

MAKING A SELF-DEFENSE DECISION

In the training world, there is an old saying that goes something like this: "In a crisis, you won't rise to the occasion. You'll fall back to the lowest level of your training."

While there are many variations of that statement, it basically means that not only will you fail to become a super-ninja warrior when you so desperately need to, you will more likely perform at a lower-than-average level. You'll only be able to count on doing things that you've done over and over, without fail, during practice. Stress, surprise and fear will all combine to diminish your cognitive capacity, and your body and brain may only reliably perform the simplest of actions that have been drilled into your subconscious by thousands of repetitions.

Certainly, this concept applies to physical response. Your ability to put shots on target or perform other self-defense actions will be limited to actions you have practiced over and over again. I always thought that a fun example of this concept is a scene in the original *Karate Kid* movie. Surrogate father and karate teacher Mr. Miyagi promises to teach young Daniel martial arts. However, the aspiring student soon finds himself waxing Miyagi's cars and painting his fence using very specific hand and arm motions. When young Daniel expresses frustration at being forced to do menial labor instead of learning karate, Miyagi launches a surprise attack on impatient young Daniel in a flurry of punches. To his great surprise, Daniel finds himself naturally blocking every thrust using the same waxing and painting motions he's been performing thousands of times on Miyagi's cars and fence. For our anxious student, the light bulb goes on, and he realizes the value of developing muscle

memory. When danger strikes, he doesn't have to think; his body simply responds because it has already done the required motion thousands of times. OK, that's Hollywood, but the concept is still valid. Do you have to think about how to balance your body on a bicycle or drink from a cup without spilling? No, you've probably done those things thousands of times, so the motions are automatic and reflexive.

But programming physical response isn't enough; you also need to think in terms of mental programming. You don't want to be making decisions with life-or-death consequences for the first time in a moment of stress, panic and fear. As with training to make physical responses automatic, you need to train your mind to take certain courses of action in advance too.

If someone suddenly pulls a knife on a loved one, do you want to be deciding whether or not you're prepared to inflict serious harm or death on that attacker? Split seconds count, so you better have made up your mind before that moment. While not fun, you need to envision a scenario in which someone is harming (or about to harm) either you or a loved one. Are you willing to kill a stranger nearly instantaneously? It may sound like a simple decision, but as much as humans are wired to fight and compete, taking a life is not something most people ever want to do. It's up to you to determine whether the pain of allowing harm to you or your family outweighs the pain of killing another.

Defensive shooting trainer and competitive shooter Michelle Cerino sums up the importance of advance mindset: "Carrying a gun has everything to do with mindset. There is nothing I will not do to protect myself and my loved ones, even if it means tak-

ing someone else's life." She has made an affirmative self-defense decision in advance.

To put this point in perspective, one needs to look no further than major wars over the past couple of centuries. There is a reason that much military training revolves around desensitization to killing and dehumanizing the enemy. That is to overcome the natural human aversion to killing one another. While studies are full of contradictions, many show that a surprising percentage of soldiers in battle either do not or will not fire at the enemy. World Wars I and II are full of stories of front-line leaders coercing their men to fire upon the enemy. Others speak to the need for officers to direct their troops to fire lower (into the enemy) as opposed to over their heads. Wherever the real data lies, the fact that these issues are so controversial still proves the point that most people are naturally disinclined to kill.

I am specifically referencing killing — the ultimate consequence. Certainly, in an ideal situation, an attacker would stop or flee when encountering resistance, but you certainly can't count on that. It's far better to assume, well in advance, that your defensive actions will result in the death of your attacker. If conflict ends in a non-lethal manner, consider it a bonus.

Advance mental work is not just about deciding whether or not you should pull the trigger. It's also important to condition your mind to the reality that a bad situation can happen to you. A friend of mine (and former SWAT Team leader), Sara Ahrens, perfectly sums up the importance of making mental decisions in advance: "What I hear from most victims or witnesses to violent crimes is regret. They regret not trusting that something didn't seem right, and they beat themselves up over it." What does this mean? When an individual sees a bad situation developing, he or she simply cannot believe that it is really happening to him or her. In his or her mind, it is so unlikely that he or she is in a life-or-death situation that precious seconds are wasted just getting to the point of accepting the current reality that he or she is in a dire circumstance. By the time he or she figures out that it really is happening, it is often too late.

The more you force your brain to go to that dark place of envisioning you or your loved ones getting caught in a defensive situation — and your response to it — the more likely you are to act quickly and decisively to protect yourself.

Is it statistically unlikely that you will become a victim of a violent crime? Thankfully yes. But, on the other hand, over three million violent crimes are committed in the United States every year. Adding to that figure, estimates indicate that another three million go unreported. The bottom line? Six million times per year, a violent crime happens. It is not out of the realm of possibility that one of those will intersect with you or your family.

When reviewing the aftermath of recent criminal attacks, you will see a broad range of responses by people present. Some will freeze. Others will go into denial. Some will spring into action, whether it be to escape or counterattack. What makes the difference? Advance planning. Those who act immediately didn't just make that decision. In advance, they considered the reality that bad stuff happens and thought about what they might do in a crisis situation. You've probably seen this phenomenon in action if you've ever witnessed a car accident. Most people will stand around contemplating the fact that they just witnessed cars crash into each other. A couple will immediately act, rushing to render aid. The odds are that the instant responders don't have any more knowledge than you or me about how to respond to a car wreck; they have just made

a conscious decision that they are going to take action. When surprised by a crisis, their brains default to a decision that has already been made: "I'm going to help."

Humans thrive on action. It's actually helpful to our psyche to make plans and commitments in advance because we like to solve problems. Now is the time to think long and hard about a few things:

1. What cues or suspicious behavior would it take for you to process that you were about to be involved in a violent crime?

2. If you become the victim of a violent encounter, are you really prepared to kill another? Make that decision now. If you aren't, don't pursue a strategy of carrying a gun for self-defense.

If you choose to make an affirmative self-defense decision, your next steps will be to support that decision with a lifetime of knowledge development and training. We'll get into those topics later.

HOMEWORK

Invest some quality time thinking about what lengths you will go to in order to protect yourself and your loved ones. Are you willing to take the life of another?

When you see crime stories on the local news, stop and imagine what you really would have done if you had been present. Would you have picked up on any clues that something bad was about to happen? Would you have been able to process the fact that a violent attack was really happening? Would you have been prepared to flee or fight on a moment's notice?

DANGERS OF A FALSE SENSE OF SECURITY

The most dangerous thing about deciding to get a gun for self-defense is the risk of living with a false sense of security. Just having a gun won't help you at all. Only the knowledge and skill of how to use it, as one of many self-defense strategies, might help you.

"Might" is the operative word. Having a gun, even with hundreds of hours of dedicated training, provides no guarantee that you will prevail if ever caught in a defensive encounter. Certainly you can improve your odds of success by developing awareness skills and strategies to implement when you see or sense that something is off. You can further improve your odds through dedication to ongoing practice and training. However, factors beyond your control, such as dumb luck and the level of determination of your attacker, will always come into play too.

Here, we are going to focus on things you can control. More importantly, we're going to talk about how you can avoid the dangers of a false sense of security. To illustrate what a false sense of security really is, consider the following scenarios.

You carry your gun in your purse, which is currently on the floor of the passenger side of your car. While driving to work, you stop to get gas. After you are finished, you are sitting in the driver seat getting ready to start your car and leave. Suddenly, the driver-side door is yanked open, a gun is put to your head, and you are given the order to move over. Does having a gun make a difference in this scenario?

You carry a gun using an undershirt holster because your office is not particularly keen on employees bringing guns to work, and you do not want to risk a fellow employee spotting your handgun. You are at a walk-up ATM. After getting some cash for lunch, you look down to put the money and receipt in your wallet. Suddenly, you feel a muzzle in your back, and someone demands your wallet and your PIN code. Does having a gun make a difference in this scenario?

You carry a small handgun using an ankle holster mainly because you prefer to tuck in your shirts and rarely wear a sports coat or jacket that could be used to cover a carry gun on your belt. When leaving a restaurant with your date, you turn the corner to the parking lot out back, only to be confronted by two thugs. One holds a gun on you while the other grabs your date. Does having a gun make a difference in this scenario?

You carry a gun using an inside-the-waistband (IWB) holster. You are in a movie theater, sitting in the middle of a row right up front, watching the latest release, when suddenly the guy in front of you stands up, turns around and starts shooting. Does having a gun make a difference in this scenario?

I paint these scenarios to bring up a point. By nature, we humans are optimistic and sometimes tend to gloss over details. When acquiring a gun for self-defense, we tend to suddenly feel empowered. After all, if there is a problem, we can just pull out our gun and solve it, right?

Well, not necessarily. Depending on whose data you use, violent encounters like those in the preceding examples are often over in just seconds — hardly enough time to get to a gun, much less put it to productive use if you are caught by surprise. What might have made a difference in these scenarios? Let's consider each from a different perspective.

While pumping your gas, you constantly scan the area around you. If you see a suspicious person who is obviously not there to fill up his car, you either go back into the store or, if distance permits, get in your car, lock it and immediately drive away. Better yet, maybe you choose to endure the inconvenience of carrying a gun on your body rather than in your purse, allowing you quicker access in case that suspicious person makes a move toward you.

Instead of getting cash at an outdoor ATM, perhaps you get cash back with your grocery purchases so you do not have to withdraw money in such an exposed environment. Or perhaps you choose always to get cash from a machine located inside of a bank branch building. While completing your transaction, you are constantly looking around to make sure no one is close enough to approach you undetected. Instead of an undershirt holster, maybe you choose a tuckable IWB or appendix holster for faster access to your gun, even using just one hand so you can use the other to fight off an attack and create distance.

Instead of parking in the back lot, you spend a few extra bucks for valet parking. Or if that is not available, maybe you discreetly walk your date around the corner in a wide arc so you can spot any lurkers around the blind corner from a safer distance. You carry a gun in a pocket or belt holster that you can access with one hand and that does not require body contortions from which to draw.

When you enter the theater before the movie, you choose a seat near the aisle, close to one of the exits. Your position allows you a better overall view of the theater and a quick means of escape if necessary.

Hopefully you can see that having or not having a gun is not the only critical factor in each of these cases. Other defensive strategies, such as planning, awareness and avoidance, are equally as important as being armed (if not more so!). While we can play "What if?" games all day with these and similar scenarios, the important takeaway is that having a gun is only a small part of an effective overall defensive strategy. Do not fall into the complacency trap of feeling safe just because you have a gun.

I think one of the best things you can do to combat a false sense of security is to create some mental scenarios when you're out and about. The idea isn't to predict some specific thing that may or may not happen but rather to get you thinking about your overall level of preparedness at any given time and place. Perhaps the easiest way to do this is to mentally role play as the mugger or aggressor. At various times and places during your daily routine, consider how you might successfully attack and then change your behavior accordingly. Here are some ideas to get you started.

When visiting an ATM, think about where you would hide if you were going to rob someone getting cash.

While waiting on your server to bring drinks at the restaurant, imagine armed robbers (or worse) barging through the front door. What would you do? Run? Hide? Drop under the table? Draw your gun and insert yourself into the situation? Do you know where the kitchen door and emergency exits are? Do you have a clear path to get out while staying out of sight of the intruders?

While driving, think about what places in your daily travels might make for ideal carjacking locations. Where are places that you stop that are a bit on the quiet side?

Do you lock your doors immediately upon getting into the car?

When entering a restaurant, think about which table has the best overall visibility of what's going on in the dining room.

When walking down the street, think about where you would hide and wait if your goal were to surprise someone.

The next time you are in a crowded public place, consider whether it is a desirable location for an attacker. What might you do to minimize risk?

You might be noticing a common theme here. Your gun is only as useful as your ability to get to it in time to make a difference. The more skill you develop with non-shooting strategies such as awareness and observation, the more likely you will be able to avoid relying on your gun. In the worst case of an unavoidable situation, you might be able to buy yourself precious seconds to put your gun into action.

Another important element of fighting a false sense of security is to think long and hard about your daily method of carry. Concealed carry is always a trade-off between concealment and gun accessibility. Generally speaking, the more concealed a gun is, the slower it is to access. While you may need to resort to less-accessible concealment methods due to the nature of your work, just enter that decision fully aware that you are sacrificing some degree of effectiveness as a trade-off.

Convenience is another trade-off that requires your brutally honest appraisal. Purse and backpack off-body carry methods

> *"The next time you're in a crowded public place, consider whether it's a location desirable for an attacker. What might you do to minimize risk?"*

are classic examples of really convenient means of concealed carry. That convenience comes at a price, however, as your gun is not in your immediate possession at all times. It can be lost or taken, leaving you unprotected or, even worse, allowing access by another.

The bottom line is this: Having a gun accomplishes very little on its own. Without a realistic plan on how you would use it, backed up by training and plenty of practice, it might be nothing more than a false sense of security.

HOMEWORK

Think through your daily routine. At what points during your regular travels is it possible for someone to catch you by surprise? Are there things you can do to change your routine or minimize the chance of a surprise violent encounter by improving your awareness?

How do you intend to carry your gun? If someone not more than a few feet away suddenly lunged at you, would your planned carry method allow you to move, fight them off and draw your gun? If not, how might you alter your carry plans? We'll get into this in far more detail later in the program. For now, just think honestly about whether your planned carry method will really help protect you.

ARE YOU GOING TO CARRY A GUN OR KEEP ONE AT HOME?

One of your first decisions will be to determine the scope of your self-defense plan. Simply put, do you intend to keep a gun solely for home defense, or do you intend to carry a concealed gun as part of a broader personal-defense plan?

Many people begin by buying a firearm and learning how to use it with the intent of keeping it at home. That is a great way to start because the barriers to entry are simpler. You can develop the skills and confidence that will allow you to migrate to concealed carry at a future date if you choose.

Let's take a look at some of the things you'll need to consider for each scenario.

KEEPING A GUN FOR HOME DEFENSE

The good news is that if you buy a gun of virtually any type for the purpose of learning how to shoot, then you've probably got something that can be used for home defense. While it may not be the ideal home-defense firearm, the odds are that it's better than a nearby frying pan. For the most part, the difference between a recreational gun and a home-defense gun boils down to how you store, feed and use it.

Purchasing and Legal Issues

Long guns (rifles and shotguns) are far less regulated than handguns. Even in restrictive states, it is relatively easy to purchase a rifle or shotgun, and the vast majority of states do not require a permit or any type of registration to purchase a long gun. Of course, you will still need to complete a National Instant Criminal Background Check System (NICS) check, but your local dealer will walk you through the process of filling out that form and getting it done.

We cannot cover all state and local laws here. Instead, we will point you to a great resource to get a handle on the laws applicable to your situation. The USCCA's

Concealed Carry Reciprocity & Gun Map (https://www.usconcealedcarry.com/ccw-reciprocity-map/) provides a fantastic overview to firearms-related laws in all 50 states.

Training and Preparation

As we discussed in the previous section, having a gun in your home accomplishes exactly nothing unless you learn how to use it for home-defense applications. Uncle Bert's old shotgun, sitting unloaded in the hall closet, is not going to help you much if someone busts down your door in the middle of the night.

For this reason, as soon as you decide to use a firearm for home defense, you'll need training. We will get you started in later chapters of this course. For now, just recognize the importance of learning the differences between recreational shooting and defending your life.

Types of Guns for Home Defense

Virtually any type of firearm can be used for home defense. That is not to say that all are equal though. There is a myriad of trade-offs to consider. A handgun is easy to maneuver but harder to shoot accurately, especially under stress. It is hard to beat a shotgun for stopping an attacker quickly, but shot capacity is limited by comparison, and recoil is not trivial. A rifle is also effective, but bullets may exit your dwelling and hit unintended targets. Many people have .22 rifles for recreational use. They're easy to shoot — and certainly lethal — but not the best for stopping an attacker quickly.

When using a firearm in the home, you'll need to think about how suitable your gun is for use in dark or low-light conditions. You'll need to think about capacity. If you hear a bump in the night, there is a good chance that your invader is not working alone, so that double-barrel shotgun's two shots may be limiting. You'll need to consider proficiency and ease of use. Are you comfortable enough operating your gun that you won't fumble with the controls in the dark?

Storing Your Home-Defense Gun

We will talk about this a lot in the next section because keeping a home-defense gun safe from children (your own or their friends) is critical. If you plan to use your gun for home defense and lock it up in a safe or cabinet to keep it away from young hands, will you still be able to access it quickly in the event of an emergency? We'll talk about storage options that allow you to keep firearms under lock and key but also accessible only to you and other authorized users.

Choosing Ammunition for Home Defense

There are more types of ammunition than cable networks, but for our purposes, you can think of two general categories of ammunition: practice and defensive.

Practice ammunition is made to go forward and punch holes in paper. Typically, for cost reasons, the bullets are made from solid lead or lead covered with copper jackets. When they hit a soft object, they will generally pass right through, making small holes with minimal damage. This is fine for the range but not for stopping a drugged-up home invader quickly. In the shotgun world, practice ammunition is comprised of tiny and light pellets that do a great job of breaking clay targets. While lethal to humans at close range, they quickly lose velocity

and penetration power 10 or more yards downrange. They will make a mess of your attacker but may not stop him in his tracks, which is the primary goal.

Defensive ammunition for handguns is designed to expand when it hits an organic target for two reasons. It makes a larger wound, increasing the odds that your attacker will stop attacking more rapidly, and it slows down faster as a side effect of this expansion, reducing the risk of a bullet exiting the target and doing damage to someone or something behind it.

CARRYING A GUN FOR SELF-DEFENSE
Purchasing and Legal Issues

If you plan to carry a gun, most states will require you to obtain a concealed carry permit. You will likely need to attend and pass a state-mandated training program and submit a detailed application that includes photo, fingerprints, proof of training and other things of that nature.

Even in states that do not require a permit for concealed carry, it is a good idea to get a permit anyway, as nearby states may honor that permit. It also can serve to identify you as one of the good folks.

Training and Preparation

If you want to carry a concealed gun for self-defense, you will need to dedicate yourself to a never-ending regimen of training (learning from qualified instructors) and practice (reinforcing learned skills on your own). Carrying a concealed gun is a commitment with life-or-death ramifications. Even if you use your concealed gun in a justified self-defense encounter, it is possible that you will be arrested. You may face charges, and you just might spend the rest of your life in jail. To minimize the risk of a tragic outcome, you will need to become an expert in self-defense law, know how to make good judgment calls and be proficient handling your firearm under stress. With rare exceptions, your state concealed carry class will prepare you for none of this, so additional training is a must.

Types of Guns for Concealed Carry

Practically speaking, concealed carry will limit you to choosing a handgun, but you can pick between a semi-automatic pistol and a revolver. There are pros and cons to each, and we'll discuss those at length in the upcoming pages. For now, you might consider these high-level pros and cons:

A revolver is simple to operate. Pull the trigger and it will go bang. There are no controls to master (with the exception of the lever that releases the cylinder when you need to reload). Most revolvers hold between five and eight rounds of ammunition before you have to reload.

A semi-automatic pistol usually has higher capacity, holding between five and 20 rounds of ammunition. Reloading is also faster, as you simply insert a fresh, pre-loaded magazine. You'll feel less recoil, as the semi-automatic operation soaks up some of the recoil impulse that you feel in your hand. On the flip side, there are more controls to master.

Choosing a Holster and Carry Method

In the "Dangers of a False Sense of Security" section, we talked about the potential pitfalls of carrying a gun in a deeply concealed or convenient way. You'll need to make some convenience and wardrobe sacrifices in order to carry a concealed gun in such a way as to make it not only safe but also accessible in a fast-evolving emergency.

We'll talk about different kinds of holsters soon. For now, understand that a good holster has to do three things:

1. Keep your gun secure so that it remains in your possession throughout your daily range of activities.

2. Keep your gun oriented correctly so that you can draw it consistently while under stress.

3. Protect the trigger to prevent unintended discharge from foreign objects.

Choosing Ammunition for Concealed Carry

As with a home-defense firearm, you'll want to understand the difference between practice and defensive ammunition. Use the inexpensive practice (full metal jacket) ammunition at the range, but swap that out for reputable self-defense ammunition before you holster your gun for concealed carry.

HOMEWORK

If you choose to buy a new gun or use an existing one for self-defense or home defense, consider the following questions:

Where are you going to store it at night?

Will it be stored in the same place during the day or when you are not at home?

What about ammunition? Will you store it nearby? Will you keep the gun loaded?

Are there others (such as children, for example) who live in your household? How will you secure the gun and ammunition from them?

Don't worry if you don't have enough information to answer all of these questions; we will be going into these topics in a lot more detail. For now, start to think about your ideal scenario. You can then make adjustments as we go.

WHAT ABOUT CHILDREN?

If you have kids in your household, or if children might visit, you will need a proactive plan for safe gun storage. By "proactive," I mean a plan that physically locks or otherwise secures your guns from unauthorized hands.

The natural tendency is to do something such as put your gun on a high shelf or maybe hide it. Storing the gun unloaded with ammunition elsewhere is a sound strategy, right? Well, actually, no. Kids, even young ones, are notoriously curious and resourceful. They'll find anything, anywhere, given enough time. Perhaps we ought to turn loose a couple of dozen 5-year-olds to find Jimmy Hoffa sometime. But seriously, more often than we should, we hear stories on the news about how a child or a visiting friend found a hidden firearm, with tragic results.

With today's affordable gun-security options, there is no excuse for anything less than properly locked and secured handgun and rifle storage.

As with any strategy, a multi-layered approach to gun safety in the home can be a good thing. Rather than relying solely on mechanical locks, it can only help to supplement that with education. After all, that's what we teach with firearms handling too. We never rely on the mechanical safety but always apply the four rules of gun safety first so that the safety devices become redundant to learned behaviors.

THE IMPORTANCE OF TRAINING

How you expose your children to guns is a personal parenting decision. Many choose to educate their children about guns, and primarily gun safety, starting at an early age. Like teaching children the dangers of sticking their fingers in a light socket or touching a hot stove, those parents want their children to understand the real danger of handling firearms without adult supervision.

Teaching safety, such as avoidance, for example, is especially important in these days of movies and video games, where kids are repeatedly desensitized to what violence is and what a firearm can do. Seeing thousands shot in video games and movies with no ill effects but rather the opposite result — entertainment — arguably removes some of the healthy fear and respect about how to handle real-life firearms.

One idea that has served many parents well is to take their kids, at the appropriate ages, to an outdoor range — not just to teach them the rules of gun safety and how to shoot safely but also to allow them to see the destructive power of a firearm firsthand. Something as simple as shooting a milk jug full of water just might help reinforce the effects of a gun shot downrange.

GUN SECURITY PRODUCTS
Gun Locks
It does not take much technology or expense to use a simple cable lock. One of these can easily disable most any firearm. While it will not protect a gun from outright theft, it does a solid job of preventing the gun's operation. Think of a cable lock as a smaller-sized bicycle lock. Just run the cable through the magazine well of a semi-automatic pistol, the cylinder of a revolver or the action of a rifle. The cable prevents the gun from closing and therefore prevents it from being fired.

If your goal is to find a safe method of storage that still allows you to access your firearm quickly in an emergency, this is not the right solution. Such a lock requires a key to open; you have to unthread the cable and then load the gun. That's too much overhead for the firearm to be immediately useful should you hear a bump in the night. If you need security from prying hands yet want to be able to use your gun for home defense, there are better solutions, although they'll cost you a little money.

The good news is that simple gun locks are readily available (and usually free). Every new gun includes one, but if you already have a firearm, you can usually pick up a free gun lock at your local police department or most any gun store. Project ChildSafe, sponsored by the National Shooting Sports Foundation, coordinates national distribution of free gun-safety kits, each of which includes a cable lock and education materials. To find a distribution partner near you, check the Project ChildSafe website at http://www.projectchildsafe.org/safety/get-a-safety-kit.

Mechanical Handgun Safes
While a cable lock binds up a firearm and prevents operation, a handgun safe completely contains the firearm in some type of locked steel box. This provides three benefits. Assuming you anchor the box to wall studs, the floor or a large piece of furniture, it provides some protection against outright theft of your handgun. Second, as the gun is contained within a locked steel box, you have protection against access from children or others who should not be handling your gun. The biggest benefit is that you can safely store your handgun in some ready or near-ready condition should you need to use it for defensive purposes.

These mechanical handgun safes are designed to lock securely yet provide quick access in an emergency. Rather than using a key or complicated combination lock that requires visibility and fine motor skills to open, many models rely on creative pattern combination locks. For example, GunVault makes various models of handgun safes that have a series of four finger depressions. Your fingers drop naturally

into the depressions, and you activate the unlocking mechanism by performing a specific pattern of button presses that you choose. The advantage to this type of lock is that you can operate it in complete darkness by touch alone. Of course, you will want to practice opening this type of lock box periodically — without looking — to make sure you can do it reliably if you are awakened from a dead sleep.

Biometric Handgun Safes

Technology has made faster solutions for rapid access simple and affordable. Now, you can buy handgun safes that are outfitted with fingerprint scanners or RFID-activated locks, there-

> *"You should be able to find an effective handgun safe for less than $100. Considering the tragic possibilities of a child accessing a gun, it's well worth the expense."*

by eliminating the need to memorize a physical lock pattern. While you can provide the combination of a physical lock to whomever you want, a biometric handgun safe allows each authorized user to have his or her own access. For example, you might set up your safe so that fingerprints from you and your spouse will open the lock. It is also a good idea to program fingerprints from each hand so that you can open the safe with either.

GunVault offers models with a fingerprint scanner and a finger touchpad for backup. Should something go wrong, it's nice to have an alternate (and nearly as fast) way to access the contents of the safe.

You also might consider an RFID handgun safe. Rather than a biometric lock such as a fingerprint scanner, this relies on a small device that electronically opens the safe when it's passed close to the lock mechanism. I have been experimenting with the Hornady Rapid Safe 2700 handgun safe. This one includes three different RFID keys that will all open the safe. You can wear a special wristband so that passing your hand over the safe will instantly unlock it. You can also use a key fob or stickers that you apply to something you already have, such as a smartphone. While RFID locks offer flexibility, it's always up to you to maintain perfect security over the RFID device that opens the lock. If you leave the wristband or key fob lying around, you haven't accomplished much. On the pro side of the equation, there is no combination to remember or scanner to operate.

Long Gun Safes and Locks

The same technology used for quick-access handgun safes is also available for rifles and shotguns. While a full-sized safe is required to completely contain the gun, quick-access solutions lock around the receiver area, discouraging movement and operation of the gun. If you anchor a unit like this into a wall, it provides a reasonable degree of theft protection, although the long gun will be in full view.

You might check out GunVault's AR-Vault as one option. It mounts on the wall and completely covers the receiver area of the rifle. Access is identical to that of GunVault handgun safes.

IN WHAT CONDITION SHOULD YOU STORE YOUR GUN?

Once you decide how you are going to secure your guns from children and other unwanted handlers, you'll need to decide in what condition you're going to store your gun. For example, will you store the locked-up gun with a round in the chamber and the safety on? Will you store the gun with a magazine inserted but no round in the chamber? If you have a pump-action shotgun, will you need to pump the action to chamber the first round? Will you store the gun completely unloaded?

These are training-issue questions that only you can answer based on your knowledge, skill and comfort level. The most important thing is to choose your method and stick to it consistently. You need to know, without doubt or hesitation, in what condition you'll find your gun when you open your safe. This is a great topic to discuss with your trainer when you attend your first class, as there are few right or wrong answers. The right method depends on your personal comfort level.

HOMEWORK

Go shopping. Most local gun stores and big-box sporting-goods retailers carry a variety of handgun and long gun safes and locking devices. You should be able to find an effective handgun safe for less than $100. Considering the tragic possibilities of a child accessing a gun, it's well worth the expense.

WHEN CAN YOU CARRY?

In most states, concealed carry is illegal without a permit. Even though you can own a gun, you probably can't carry it around with you. There are exceptions, as a number of states support "constitutional carry." This means that no permit is required to own a handgun or to carry one on your person. Constitutional carry states take the text of the Second Amendment as it reads: "The right to keep and bear arms shall not be infringed."

As of 2018, a handful of states have some form of constiutional carry. But don't rely on this book or any other; always check your local laws directly, as things often change quickly in the world of firearms. A good resource is the USCCA's Concealed Carry Reciprocity Map & State Gun Laws site, found at https://www.usconcealedcarry.com/ccw-reciprocity-map/. Remember that you are the one ultimately responsible for knowing and following the laws in your area.

You will find variations on carrying a gun without a permit. True constitutional carry states will allow for either concealed or open (exposed and visible) carry without a special permit, though some states specify this flexibility for residents only. Other states may allow open carry without a special permit but require a state-issued concealed carry permit to legally carry concealed.

Depending on what day it is, as many as 45 states allow some form of open carry. More accurately, you might think of this as 45 states not currently prohibiting open carry. Within these states, you'll find a broad range of technicalities. Some states allow open carry of long guns and handguns. Others allow long guns only. Others allow handguns but not long guns.

Some require that openly carried guns be unloaded. The whole open carry debate is a political hot potato, so be sure to keep up with your own state's position on the matter if you choose to exercise that right.

We are not going to get into the political debate over whether open carry is a good idea or not. Instead, we will focus on a purely defensive perspective. If your goal is to carry openly for convenience or political reasons, knock yourself out. If your goal is to protect yourself and your family, then think long and hard about whether you should carry openly. Carrying an exposed gun takes one of your primary advantages off the table: Bad guys do not know that you are armed, so you have complete control over whether or not you engage in an active self-defense situation. I get that some believe in the deterrence aspect of open carry, but my strong preference is to keep my armed status to myself, only revealing that at a time and place of my choosing — not that of an attacker. This is another great topic to discuss with your training class instructor.

FEDERAL LAWS AND RESTRICTIONS

While most federal firearms laws are concerned with commerce related to firearms, there are some federal regulations that affect where you can carry. Most of these restrictions involve carry policy on various types of federal property. For example, carry is prohibited in federal courthouses, most federal buildings, federal prisons, military bases, national cemeteries and post offices. For a more detailed list, you can check the USCCA's Concealed Carry Reciprocity Map listed in the homework section at the end of this chapter.

STATE LAWS AND RESTRICTIONS

The vast majority of concealed carry law resides at the state level. Be sure to determine whether your state has a preemption law, meaning that state law related to guns applies statewide, and localities within the state cannot make their own firearms-related laws. Without state preemption, counties and cities can make their own laws regarding carry and gun regulations, making it impossible for residents to know what is legal and what is not as they go about their daily business. A simple 10-mile drive within the same state might create conflicting regulations. If your state does not have preemption, you will need to check local ordinances and be aware of the regulations of other cities and counties you visit.

On Your Person

Whether you may or may not carry a gun around on your person, either concealed or openly, depends entirely on the laws of your particular state. Outside of the states that embrace permitless or constitutional carry and states where open carry is legal, you will almost always need a state-issued permit or a valid permit from another state with a reciprocity agreement. We will get to that in a minute. The bottom line is this: Be very sure you understand the laws of your state (and city or county, if applicable) before carrying a gun on your person.

While you can often carry a gun without a permit depending on where you live, it is almost always a good idea to go ahead and get a state permit anyway. In some cases, having a permit expands the list of places where you can legally carry. A permit may also give you carry status in other states. Last, it is a stake in the ground that identifies you as one of the good guys.

Carrying in Your Car

States also have widely differing laws on keeping a gun in your car. There is more flexibility to do this without having a concealed carry permit than there is to carry a gun on your person. Just be aware that every state has different regulations regarding keeping a gun in your car. Some states require the gun to be hidden out of sight. Other states require the exact opposite. For example, in North Carolina, you cannot carry a gun in an unlocked glove compartment without a concealed carry permit. However, you can display your gun openly on the seat (in theory) or store it in a locked glove compartment. In South Carolina, anyone who can legally own a gun can carry one loaded, provided it is in the glove compartment, console or trunk. Every state has its own way of doing things, and laws change on a regular basis in today's political climate, so check the website listed at the end of this chapter and your state's own sites to keep current on applicable laws.

Firearms Owners' Protection Act

No federal permit is required to transport your firearms across state lines, provided you can legally own and carry a gun at your point of origin and your final destination. That means that if you can own and carry a gun in Florida and are traveling to Maine, where you are also legal to own and carry a firearm, you have (in theory) safe passage between those two points.

The Firearms Owners' Protection Act clarifies this process and sets basic guidelines on the proper way to transport your gun while in transit. For example, the gun must not only be unloaded but also completely out of reach, such as in your trunk. If your vehicle does not have a trunk, the gun must be in a locked container and unloaded.

While this legislation was intended to protect innocent travelers from overzealous prosecution while passing through gun-unfriendly states, there has still been harassment. Periodically, you'll hear a story on the news about an unwitting traveler getting arrested in states such as Maryland, New Jersey or New York, regardless of the protection offered by the Firearms Owners' Protection Act. The bottom line is that these states have many more lawyers than you can afford. Knowing that you cannot defend yourself, they have been known to prosecute anyway. Thankfully, abuses like this are not everyday occurrences, but they do happen. The best thing you can do is to plan your routes accordingly.

Concealed Carry Permits

As previously mentioned, taking the time to acquire a state-issued concealed carry permit is almost always a good idea. Your state will likely have a long list of places where you can't legally carry, so be sure you know what those are. On that list, you're likely to find places such as schools, churches, bars, government buildings and others.

It is also a good idea to understand your state's laws regarding "no guns allowed" signage. Businesses and organizations may be able to post signs that prohibit lawful concealed carriers from entering their premises while carrying.

Different states apply different forces of law to these sign policies. In some states, it is a serious offense with real consequences. Other states don't put much force of law behind a willful violation of the sign policy. Before you make a decision as to how you will handle locations with signage, be sure you understand the consequences. The safest solution is always to avoid these businesses. Be sure to call later and let them know they lost your business because of the signs. Tell them you couldn't enter their establishments because their signs stopped you, a law-abiding citizen, at their doors. Oh, and be sure to remind them that their signs never stop criminals.

State Reciprocity

One of the benefits of getting a concealed carry permit is that many states honor other states' carry permits. For example, I have a South Carolina concealed weapons permit. Because I have this, certain other states will allow me to carry concealed because they have reciprocity agreements with South Carolina. The USCCA website will give you up-to-date information on reciprocity agreements between your state and others.

HOMEWORK

Visit the following website to learn as much as you can about your local laws regarding open and concealed carry of firearms:

https://www.usconcealedcarry.com/ccw-reciprocity-map/

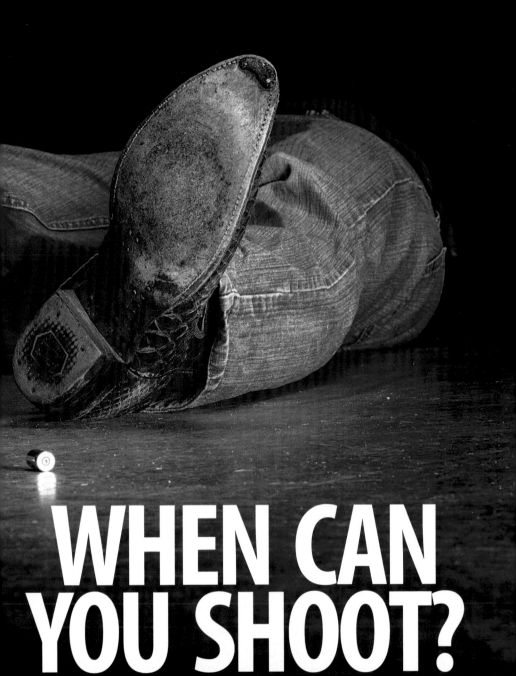

WHEN CAN YOU SHOOT?

Knowing, really knowing, exactly what circumstances might justify the act of shooting someone in self-defense has life-changing ramifications. If you do have to shoot in self-defense, it's not guaranteed that you'll get the benefit of the doubt. In fact, you'll probably be held to a ridiculous standard. Prosecutors (and possibly jurors) will spend days, weeks or even months carefully evaluating the actions you had to take in a split second. They'll have the luxury of time to ponder, second-guess and Monday-morning-quarterback your actions. Unfair? Perhaps, but that's how it is.

Just this morning, I read a story about a Canadian police officer who shot a suspect armed with a knife. The assailant drew a knife and moved toward the officer. The officer issued commands to "stop" and "drop the knife." He even shouted that he would have to shoot if the perpetrator didn't stop advancing. Unfortunately, the officer was not equipped with a Taser, so he didn't have a non-lethal alternative available. That's beside the point, as someone was advancing on him with a lethal weapon. I only mention it to highlight the difficulty of the officer's situation. Finally, the officer had to fire to stop the attacker; he shot the man three times. The man fell backward and was on his back on the ground when he started reaching for the knife again. The officer, almost certainly facing tunnel vision and target fixation (as is normal in a stressful situation), fired multiple more times, killing the assailant. Later, the officer was charged with murder — twice! First, he faced a second-degree murder charge for the first three shots, even though he was defending himself against a knife-wielding attacker. Since some seconds went by before the fallen assailant went for his knife again, the officer was charged with murder — again — for the second series of shots he fired. This time, the charge was murder in the first degree. Prosecutors and the press vilified this officer, claiming that since the assailant was on his back, he was no longer a threat, even though he had grabbed the knife again. It's nice to have such hindsight, isn't it? Of course, the second-guessers weren't there, probably had never faced a lethal attack and knew nothing of deadly force encounters and the associated physiological factors. I hope that the police department provides the officer a defense attorney smart enough to walk the jury through physiological responses such as tunnel vision. I wasn't there either, but it wouldn't surprise me to learn that the officer's brain, as a result of extreme stress, was fixated on the knife. When he saw the guy grab the knife, he fired again in self-defense.

I tell this story not to try that officer's story in the pages of this book but to illustrate what happens far too often. Ill-informed people will reflect, from the comfort of their televisions and office chairs, upon the actions you should have taken in the span of a few fractions of a second while literally fighting for your life. It's a lousy deal, but that's what it is. It's also the reason why it's so important for every gun owner to understand exactly what the laws are for concepts such as self-defense, "stand your ground" and the Castle Doctrine.

There are more than 20,000 gun laws on the books nationwide, and that doesn't even count non-gun-related laws covering broader concepts such as homicide, self-defense, "stand your ground" and the Castle Doctrine. There are more laws than you could ever possibly know, but by law, you're required to abide by them. Not knowing about any given law is not a valid defense. The best you can do is thoroughly understand the underlying principles of self-defense.

At a high level, I like Massad Ayoob's definition of a justifiable self-defense shooting. As a police officer who has trained tens of thousands of people over decades and who has testified as an expert witness in countless courtrooms, he's learned a thing or two. His definition of justifiable self-defense is this: "Deadly force is justified only when undertaken to prevent imminent and otherwise unavoidable danger of death or grave bodily harm to the innocent."

To understand the concept more fully, we need to consider the elements that make up a justifiable self-defense shooting. These are the factors that the Monday-morning quarterbacks will evaluate at their leisure, even though you had to make your decision under extreme stress in a fraction of a second.

At the highest level, a jury will evaluate your actions based on what a "reasonable person" would have done under the exact same set of circumstances. Assuming the jury is comprised of reasonable people, they will look at your case, pretend to know what you knew at the time and determine if they would have taken the same or similar action. Even the reasonable person doctrine is a bit of a stretch because they now know more than you knew at the time. They know the end result, and they've had the luxury of time to contemplate all the other things you could have done. Even still, they're supposed to put themselves in your shoes to determine if whatever you did was reasonable.

Thankfully, the legal system provides more structure to help others determine if your actions were consistent with those of a reasonable person. Those in charge of evaluating your actions will consider three elements to determine if your shooting was justified under the law: ability, opportunity and jeopardy. Let's take a look at each.

Ability

If you shoot someone in self-defense, the attacker must have had the ability to inflict grave bodily harm or death. While the news media likes to make a big deal about unarmed attackers, that's not relevant under the law. Those attackers' ability to inflict harm is what matters.

Consider a slightly silly example. Let's assume you weigh 95 pounds and can bench-press a grand total of 25 pounds. Bruce Lee's evil twin attacks you with nothing but his bare hands. Does he have the ability to inflict grave bodily harm or death on you? Absolutely yes. Now bring that to a more realistic scenario. What if an experienced, 250-pound street-fighting ex-con attacks your 15-year-old daughter, again without a weapon? Does he have the ability to inflict grave bodily harm? Again, absolutely yes. Under the correct interpretation of legal principles, who has what weapon does not matter. If someone can inflict grave bodily harm or death on you, you can be justified in using lethal force to defend yourself.

Of course, the court of public opinion will not consider such things. It will rant about you shooting an unarmed assailant. You'll have to prove, to a prosecutor or in a courtroom, that your attacker had the ability to inflict death or grave bodily harm.

Opportunity

The next element that needs to be met is opportunity. In our previous example, if evil Bruce Lee was 15 miles away from his victim, he had the ability to inflict harm, but not the opportunity. Obviously, if your assailant is threatening you via email from 100 miles away, you can't shoot in self-defense. In most cases, proximity is the big factor when it comes to establishing opportunity. Was the assailant close enough to you to inflict harm?

Jeopardy

The final element is jeopardy. Was your life or physical well-being in jeopardy? Just because a 250-pound ex-con who has the ability to harm you is standing nearby does not necessarily mean you are in jeopardy. Is that person displaying behavior that a reasonable person would interpret as harmful? Certainly, if your attacker is actively trying to beat you to death or is shooting at you, jeopardy is established. If he or she is saying mean things, not so much.

Interestingly, the case mentioned earlier about the Canadian police officer will likely center around the jeopardy element. The attacker, with a knife, had the ability to harm. He was dangerously close, so the opportunity criteria was met. In the first volley of shots, few would argue that the officer wasn't in jeopardy. After the knife-wielding assailant was on the ground, the question of jeopardy becomes difficult to discern.

While not one of the three definitional elements, you also need to consider innocence. If you're robbing a bank, and the armed guard has the ability and opportunity to put your life in jeopardy, you won't be able to mount a successful justifiable self-defense campaign. Why? You weren't innocent. You were breaking the law. That's one of the reasons why responsible concealed carriers do everything humanly possible to avoid conflict. When you're carrying a gun, you don't want to win any arguments with strangers. You want to smile, tell them to have a nice day and walk away.

When you shoot someone, you are committing homicide. It might be justifiable, and we're going to talk about that in the next segment, but the tables are turned when you fire in self-defense. You start out as guilty and have to prove your innocence. That's why it's so important to understand and internalize the concepts of justifiable self-defense now — before you have to make a split-second life-or-death decision.

HOMEWORK

Every time you see a story on the news or read an account of an armed citizen's action against a criminal, dissect the story through the courtroom lens of ability, opportunity and jeopardy. While you may agree with the armed citizen's actions, take an objective look at the facts reported to see if and how each element of justifiable self-defense was met.

Likewise, the next time a story about a law enforcement officer shooting an unarmed assailant becomes national news, consider the three elements of justifiable self-defense to see if you agree with the prevailing opinion.

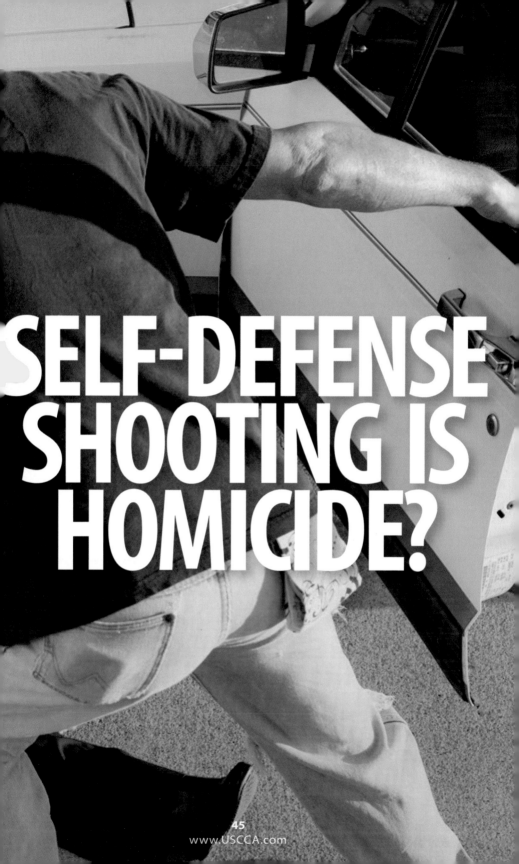

SELF-DEFENSE SHOOTING IS HOMICIDE?

Yes, shooting and killing someone else, even in self-defense, is a homicide. Does that surprise you? Good. Because it's an important concept that we all need to understand. Police will investigate the incident to determine if the shooting was a justifiable act of self-defense and therefore protected from future prosecution.

Even if your actions were justified, a person is dead because of those actions. It's hard to argue with that, right? You've survived. The other person has not.

Here's where things get interesting. You've clearly committed homicide, which is normally a felony of the highest degree. Yet there were extenuating circumstances that drove your actions. In fact, in an unchallenged self-defense scenario, you may have had no choice but to commit homicide against your attacker. Under the law, in a situation like this, your actions can be excusable, thereby relieving you from the consequences of committing a homicide.

In the USCCA book *Armed and Ready, Your Comprehensive Blueprint to Concealed Carry Confidence,* I explain the concept with this analogy:

If 007 were visiting our fine country and ran a red light while preventing Goldfinger from setting off a nuclear explosion at Fort Knox, the act of run-

> *"One of the reasons that understanding the concept of affirmative defense is so important is that it impacts your entire legal-defense strategy should you suffer the misfortune of getting involved in a self-defense shooting."*

ning the red light would still have been illegal. However, if secret agent James Bond had not run the red light, millions of people may have been harmed or killed, and the movie would have had a very sad ending. The extenuating circumstances excuse the consequences of his unlawful behavior. There is no law that states that it is legal to run a red light if the driver is under time duress to prevent a nuclear explosion that would contaminate the country's gold reserves for tens of thousands of years. On the contrary, there IS a provision in the law to excuse illegal behavior under very specific circumstances.

Getting back to self-defense, the armed citizen who commits homicide in self-defense has the legal tables turned on him or her. Rather than a presumption of innocence until proven guilty, he or she is, in practical terms, guilty until proven innocent. After all, someone is dead; there's no disputing that. To clear himself or hersellf of the charge of murder, the armed citizen must admit to the homicide and mount what legal eagles refer to as an "affirmative defense."

At the risk of butchering legal terminology, think of an affirmative defense as an admission of guilt — but with an expression of extenuating circumstance. "Yes, I did shoot the thug who was trying to kill me, but I had no choice but to defend myself and/or others, and a rational person would have done the exact same thing in the same circumstance, knowing what I knew at the time." The ultimate goal of such an affirmative defense is a ruling of "justifiable homicide." That is the phrase which releases the armed citizen from the normal penalty for homicide. After all, the homicide was only committed in the interest of the greater good, preventing death or grave bodily harm.

One of the reasons that understanding the concept of affirmative defense is so important is that it affects your entire legal-defense strategy should you suffer the misfortune of getting involved in a self-defense shooting. In a typical criminal trial, when the defendant is often guilty, strategies range from denial and casting of doubt on the defendant's actions to finding procedural technicalities that might negate the charge. In other words, the defense attorney may be doing everything in his or her power to duck, dodge and avoid the accusations of the crime. In an affirmative defense, most armed citizens will benefit from a knowledgeable attorney who's more accustomed to the prosecutorial side, where offense is the underlying strategy.

In the previous chapter, "When Can You Shoot?," the case of the Canadian police officer is one that will likely rely on the legal strategy of presenting an affirmative defense in an attempt to seek a ruling of justifiable homicide. I suspect that the officer's legal team will try to show that, even though the suspect was already down on the ground, he was still trying to inflict harm with

his knife, hence the officer's second shooting response.

The takeaway from this chapter is to understand that your legal defense, should you ever have the misfortune of finding yourself justifying your self-defense actions, will be flipped on its head. You may very well be presumed guilty until you can justify your actions. Certainly, in an obvious self-defense situation, law enforcement and the prosecutor may realize right off the bat that your actions represented clear justifiable homicide. In that event, charges may never be pressed. However, all too often, an aggressive prosecutor looking to make a case will pursue prosecution, even if your actions were correct.

HOMEWORK

Check out some of the many true stories of self-defense situations and results on the USCCA's website. The following section contains hundreds of real-life articles: https://www.usconcealedcarry.com/category/true-stories/. Try to evaluate the stories from a perspective of justifiable homicide.

PLANNING FOR YOUR WORST LEGAL NIGHTMARE

A smart armed citizen will always do everything in his or her power, and I mean everything, to avoid ever having to fire his or her concealed handgun at someone else. Why? There are no good outcomes … ever. The best possible outcome if you ever shoot someone is that you and your loved ones escape physical injury or death. That sounds great, but it all too often comes at great cost, starting with the fact that you injured or killed someone.

What seems like the end of your major problems is just the beginning. That's because your legal battle begins immediately after you dial 911. Every action you took will be scrutinized, evaluated and second-guessed, and you'll have to explain your actions sufficiently to avoid a homicide or attempted-murder prosecution.

Here are some of the things you might expect and some ideas on what you can do to prepare.

In the event you are caught in a self-defense encounter, even if no shots are fired, call 911 and report the incident as quickly as you can from a safe location. You always want to be the first to report an incident, as you'll be the one presumed innocent while facts are being gathered. If you ever have to draw a gun to prevent an attack, there's nothing to prevent the attacker from calling the police and claiming that some crazy person threatened him with a gun. Always call first.

If the encounter ended in gunfire and either injury or death, still call 911 immediately, but report the basic facts only. Don't try to relate the entire incident over the phone. The vast majority of people coming out of a high-adrenaline encounter haven't yet processed exactly what happened, so your odds of reporting details accurately are very low. Remember, you'll be judged later on every word you say, so take the time to calm down and make sure you are mentally able to relate the facts accurately and completely. Very few people — police officers or armed citizens — can recall something as simple as the number of shots they fired. Don't try when you're in an agitated state.

Prepare for the arrival of law enforcement. Be sure to describe yourself to the 911 operator or, better yet, have someone else do it. Be sure you're ready to holster or otherwise secure your gun as police arrive. Remember, they don't yet know what happened and who is the criminal and who is the victim. Make their job easier and safer by cooperating fully and immediately with any commands.

You may or may not be handcuffed and arrested. Your gun will most likely be taken, as it's now evidence. That's OK. The police officers are doing their job, securing the scene and gathering the evidence. There will be plenty of time later to tell your story.

When it comes to talking to responding police about what happened, be accurate, straightforward and helpful, but be wary about trying to relate too many details. Remember, your brain probably has not processed all those details, and relaying incorrect information will harm your case later. Feel free to tell the officers that you are upset and need some time to decompress but that you want to cooperate fully. There is conflicting advice about how much to talk with officers until your lawyer is present. No one can answer that, as every situation is different, so you'll have to make a judgment call. It will probably benefit you to err on the side of caution by talking less rather than more until you fully process the event in

your mind. Your natural instinct will be to be as helpful as possible and talk about everything in detail. You're innocent, after all. But right then, you might be the only one who knows that, and you don't want to incriminate yourself by blabbing uncontrollably and inaccurately.

We should pause here to emphasize some of the reasons why you need to be very careful in how quickly you start to tell the details of your encounter. Under extreme stress, the human body does all sorts of strange things. While these physiological and mental responses are protective mechanisms geared to help you in a fight-or-flight response, they're not particularly helpful when it comes to mounting a detailed legal defense.

Under extreme stress, you'll likely experience basic physical responses, such as diversion of blood from small muscle groups to big muscle groups. Fight or flight doesn't rely so much on finger dexterity as it does on the large muscles in the legs and arms. You might also experience tunnel vision. Your brain will zero in on the threat and exclude everything else going on in your normal peripheral vision. You may even experience auditory exclusion. Many people who fire shots in self-defense recall not hearing their shots at all. That's because your brain shuts off those inputs, as they are not deemed important to your immediate survival. Others report time dilation, where events appear to be taking place in slow motion. In other words, your brain, to present and process only the information it deems critical to immediate survival, filters and excludes a lot of information that officers and lawyers will want to know. Now do you see why you

want to be careful about trying to relay too much information? If you can't even hear your shots, and your brain is on filter mode, how are you going to know how many shots you fired? In fact, most people report shooting far fewer times than they actually did. Imagine how that will sound to a jury later. Remember, they'll be analyzing all these things after the fact, without all the diminished mental capacity that you endured during a fight for your life.

If you are arrested, it will be beneficial if you already have a relationship with a local attorney experienced in self-defense law. Better yet, consider joining a program such as the USCCA Self-Defense SHIELD, referenced in today's homework section. If your event occurs during off hours, a program such as this will have a 24-hour hotline, whereas a local attorney may be difficult to reach immediately. You might consider calling your spouse or significant other so he or she can begin to coordinate resources on your behalf. Be sure to tell him or her that you are OK and in police custody (name the specific officer, if possible), and instruct him or her to start taking action on the plan you've hopefully discussed in advance.

Additional actions might include searches of your home and confiscation of any other firearms you have. Law enforcement's job is to figure out what happened by gathering evidence and interviewing witnesses, so don't be offended that they may not take your word as to the exact sequence of events.

Be patient and cooperative through all this. It's a normal part of the process, and, in most cases in which an armed citizen took appropriate self-defense action, the facts quickly sort themselves out. Just this week, I watched a cellphone video in which, while a man was holding a carjacker at gunpoint, the police arrived and shook the armed citizen's hand. They're on your side; just be cooperative and help them do their job.

HOMEWORK

From this point on, take notes of every bit of training you receive related to concealed carry and self-defense. Ideally, get a separate notebook just for this purpose and carefully date each class you complete, providing information on the instructor and notes from the lessons. If you are ever challenged as to why you took certain actions, you want to be the party who took it upon himself or herself to become trained. You'll want to be able to back up your actions with what you were taught to do.

This is also a great time to begin exploring legal resources that might help you in the aftermath of a self-defense encounter. Check out the resources available to you with a USCCA membership. The Self-Defense SHIELD offers legal and financial protection after a self-defense incident and connects you with the USCCA's Critical Response Team.

WHAT DO GUNS ACTUALLY DO?

Guns don't knock people off their feet or send them flying through plate-glass windows (unless you're stuck in a Hollywood B movie).

What guns really do is make relatively small holes, accompanied by concussion and noise. Don't get me wrong, it's an ugly process, and those holes are made in a destructive and dramatic way, but there's nothing particulary magical about a gun (especially a handgun). It simply allows the user to project the hole-making capability at a safer distance from his or her attacker.

We'll get into the reasons why in a minute, but for now, it's important to understand that shooting someone is not likely to knock him off his feet and immediately stop whatever bad thing he is doing. It might, but the "one-shot stop" is the exception, not the rule. In fact, most shootings require between two and three shots, on average, to stop an attacker. Sometimes, determined attackers who are amped up on rage or chemicals can endure an astounding number of shots before giving up.

Consider the 1986 Miami shootout in which eight FBI agents engaged serial bank robbers Michael Platt and William Matix. The gunfight lasted nearly five minutes and involved 145 rounds in total. Matix was hit six times before he stopped fighting, while Platt was hit 12 times before he was subdued.

In November 2006, three Pennsylvania police officers were ambushed by a single assailant. The attacker absorbed six shots from .40-caliber pistols loaded with hollow-point ammunition and 11 shots from .223 AR-15 rifles before the fight was over. After suffering 17 gunshot wounds, the subject had to be physically wrestled to be cuffed and arrested. He died eventually but clearly continued to fight through an astounding number of pistol and rifle hits.

In Los Angeles, a suspect continued to fire at officers after being shot 20 times. In another encounter, a suspect was shot 33 times before he stopped fighting. Both criminals suffered mortal wounds; they just didn't know it and continued to inflict harm.

On the other hand, some gunfights end after a single shot. Why the big difference? Let's discuss that in more detail.

THE 'KNOCKDOWN POWER' MYTH

When evaluating handguns and ammunition, many people talk about "knockdown power." In the technical sense, this whole idea is a myth. Handguns don't have knockdown power. If a handgun bullet had enough momentum (not energy; we'll clarify the difference in a minute) to knock over someone it hit, then the shooter would be knocked down as well. That's Newton's Third Law of Motion in action.

You'll also hear the term "stopping power." That's a different idea and refers to the ability of a round to stop someone from doing what he's doing. An attacker may stop whatever bad thing he's doing for a number of reasons, even if he doesn't get physically knocked over by the momentum of a bullet.

ENERGY AND MOMENTUM

At the risk of oversimplifying very complicated physics, you might think of a bullet as having two measurements of power: energy and momentum.

Energy is commonly shown on boxes of ammunition in units of foot-pounds. A 9mm defensive round may have 350 or 400 foot-pounds of energy. This figure is derived from the weight of the bullet and its velocity. Think of this kinetic-energy measurement as the amount of destructive power the bullet has on tissue, not its ability to move an object. Maybe a high-speed drill bit offers an analogy: Putting one in a bowl of jello will cause chaos for sure because there is a lot of non-directional energy at play, but it's not going to knock the bowl across the room.

Momentum is also derived from mass and velocity but is a more accurate measurement of the ability to move something. If you hang a bowling ball from the ceiling, pull it back, then let it swing into the bowl of jello, it's going to send that dessert dish flying.

Handgun and rifle bullets have enormous kinetic energy but not nearly as much momentum. That's why they don't physically knock people off their feet — at least not as a result of momentum.

HOW RIFLES ARE DIFFERENT

With rifles, things start to get interesting, and the simple effects of kinetic energy and momentum are more blurred. At the relatively low velocity of a handgun bullet, usually in the 1,000-feet-per-second range (give or take a couple of hundred feet), the bullet will cause significant (but not explosive) tissue damage. As the bullet passes through tissue, the flesh expands out of the way, then contracts back toward its original configuration. Ballistic nerds refer to this as a "temporary wound channel."

The permanent wound channel remains relatively small. That's the reason people describe handgun bullets as making small holes.

A rifle bullet typically moves at three times (give or take) the velocity of a handgun bullet. Due to the extreme velocity involved, usually well over 2,000 feet per second, tissue moves out of the way at a rate far greater than it can handle. Rather than stretching and bouncing back, tissue tends to be permanently destroyed. That's one of the reasons why a relatively small rifle bullet can cause so much damage.

HOW GUNS ACTUALLY STOP PEOPLE

To keep things simple, let's consider the question of how handguns stop people since rifles are in a different class when it comes to stopping power.

We've already established that a bullet does not have enough momentum to knock someone off his or her feet, yet sometimes a person getting shot stops attacking, falls down, drops, jumps or something else altogether. Why? There could be a number of reasons.

Factors could be mental, physical, structural or even electrical. Let's consider a few of them, not in any particular order of effectiveness.

Fear is a big driving factor for us humans. It's a healthy emotion designed to keep us away from trouble and harm. When some people are on the receiving end of a big noise, flash, concussion or bullet impact, fear may be enough to encourage them to give up the fight right then and there. After all, how many of us want to get shot again? Once is more than a lifetime's worth for most rational people.

On a related note, pain is a great motivator to stop someone from continuing his attack. Some gunshot recipients have enough of the pain after the first shot or two and decide to throw in the towel.

Sometimes, it's structural damage that stops a determined attacker. There are hundreds of cases of people getting shot multiple times yet continuing to fight. However, depending on the location of a bullet's impact, structural damage may make it impossible to continue to fight. If an attacker's pelvis is shattered, he won't be able to stand up and fight no matter how much he wants to. Certainly, if armed with his own gun, he can fight from the ground, but the lack of bone structure won't allow much mobility.

Neurological damage is another way that a handgun bullet can stop a fight. Damage to the brain or the spinal cord can simply shut down the body's electrical system — usually instantly. One shot to a vital electrical area can end a fight, while many shots to less essential parts of the body might have a less visible effect.

The final thing that stops people is the loss of blood pressure. Bullets make holes, and — depending on where the hits impact — those holes result in blood loss. A hit to the heart or a major artery results in very rapid blood loss, preventing the body from functioning after about 20 seconds or so.

Hits to other areas may not cause enough blood loss to slow one down for several minutes or more. Barring direct neurological damage, blood loss over time is the leading cause of death from gunshot wounds.

WHAT DOES THIS ALL MEAN?

As you can see, there are myriad factors at play when it comes to gunshot wounds. An important thing to learn from the experience of others is that lethality and stopping capability are two often unrelated things. A single shot from a small .22 LR bullet may kill an attacker, but if it takes five minutes to do so, that's not going to help you while you're being attacked. On the other hand, a single shot to a structural or neurological zone may stop an attack instantly, even if it doesn't kill the attacker.

The goal of shooting in self-defense isn't to kill; it's to stop the attack as quickly as possible. There are too many tragic stories in which, even after suffering a mortal wound, attackers still continue to fight and inflict harm before they expire. That's why it's important to understand that your objective in a self-defense shooting is to stop your attacker. That might take one shot or 10 — you never know.

HOMEWORK

Read the following articles to continue your education on stopping power:

https://www.usconcealedcarry.com/on-calibers-guns-and-stopping-power/

https://www.usconcealedcarry.com/ballistic-bs/

https://www.usconcealedcarry.com/self-defense-ammo-the-search-for-the-magic-bullet/

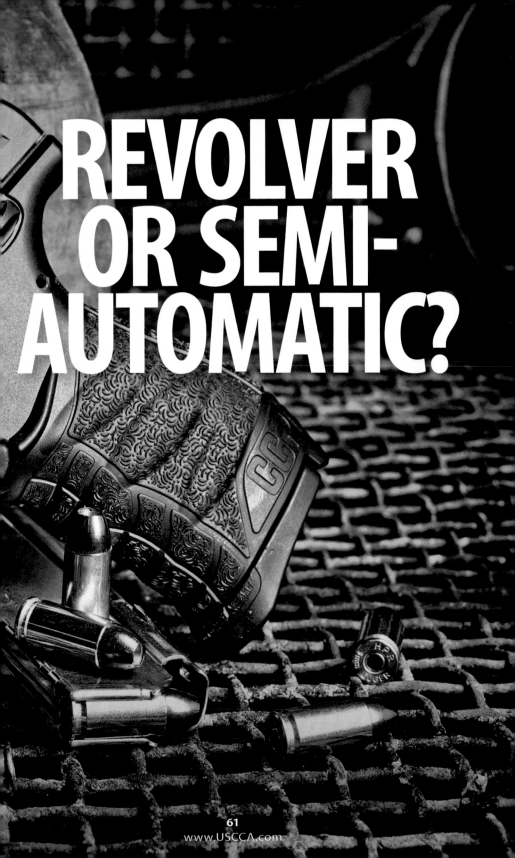

REVOLVER OR SEMI-AUTOMATIC?

When it comes to choosing the type of gun you'll use for concealed carry (revolver or semi-automatic pistol), there's good news: Either is just fine. It's far more important to choose a gun with which you're comfortable and can accurately shoot.

To help make your decision, let's review the differences between the two most common types of handguns. Before we get into those, know that there are other types of handguns that can be used for self-defense. The most popular of the other types is a derringer-style gun. As this type only fires once or twice before a reload is required, I generally wouldn't recommend it as a primary carry gun.

If you want to understand the technical difference between a revolver and a pistol, you need to understand the concept of chambers. A chamber is the portion of a barrel that holds the cartridge just prior to firing.

In a semi-automatic, the chamber is physically part of the overall barrel. The interior of the barrel is cut to the proper shape to hold the cartridge that the pistol is designed to fire. Just before firing, a cartridge is loaded into the chamber area of the barrel. After the cartridge is fired, the now-empty cartridge case is extracted from the chamber to make room for another cartridge. This happens automatically, hence the name "semi-automatic." The pistol fires only once for each trigger pull; it's just the self-reloading capability for the next cartridge that's automatic.

A revolver has multiple chambers that are not physically part of the barrel. Instead, the chambers are machined into a steel cylinder, and a cartridge is loaded into each chamber at once. As the cylinder rotates, each chamber lines up with the barrel, allowing its cartridge to fire. The empty cartridge case stays in place as the next cartridge is rotated into alignment with the barrel.

I get into the technical differences because they make a difference regarding both operation and ammunition capacity. The capacity of a revolver is limited by the size of the cylinder and the number of chambers. To fit more cartridges, the revolver's cylinder has to be larger. For an average revolver cartridge, such as the .38 Special, you'd need a really large-diameter cylinder to hold more than six or eight rounds at a time. Most revolvers hold five or six rounds, but some go to seven or eight. For really small cartridges such as .22 LR, you can fit more in the same space, so you'll find revolvers that hold 10 or so rounds of that cartridge.

REVOLVERS: PROS AND CONS

Revolvers are very simple to operate. If all of the chambers are loaded, the operation is straightforward. Just pull the trigger and the hammer will fall on the cartridge currently in position. On a double-action revolver, the trigger pull also rotates the cylinder, so cartridges line up with barrel as you fire them. There are no extra controls to master. The only control besides the trigger is a latch that unlocks the cylinder so you can empty spent cartridge cases and load new cartridges.

As hinted earlier, one of the cons to choosing a revolver is capacity. After you fire five or six rounds, you'll need to reload. This brings up another con when compared to semi-automatic pistols: Reloading a revolver is slower and requires more manual dexterity.

After expending the spent cases, you must insert a new cartridge into each chamber. You may use speedloading tools that hold the cartridges to match up with the chambers so you can drop all five or six into position at once.

PISTOLS: PROS AND CONS

The most obvious benefit of a semi-automatic pistol is ammunition capacity relative to the overall size of the gun. Since cartridges are stored in a magazine inserted into the grip, you can fit a lot of them in the gun without significantly increasing size. Depending on the dimensions of the pistol, capacity might range from six or seven at the very lowest end to 20 at the high end for a full-sized model.

Reloading is also fast and easy with a pistol. When a magazine is empty, a button press will eject the entire magazine; you can then insert a fresh one pre-loaded with cartridges. With a little bit of practice, you can easily fully reload a pistol in less than a second.

Another benefit to a semi-automatic pistol is that it has less perceptible recoil than a revolver of similar weight shooting a cartridge of similar power. Some of the recoil energy is redirected into the mechanical action of ejecting the spent cartridge case and reloading a new one. All of the recoil energy is still there, but it feels softer because a portion has been redirected.

On the con side, a semi-automatic pistol is more complex to operate. Depending on the specific type of action, there might be a manual safety, a decocking lever, a magazine release lever and a slide release lever. Regular practice will make operating these controls second nature, but the fact remains that there is more to know when operating a pistol rather than a revolver.

TYPES OF ACTIONS

Handguns operate in a variety of modes. Let's take a quick look at how each works so can you make a more informed decision about what's best for you.

Single-Action

A single-action firearm does one thing when you press the trigger: It releases a pre-cocked hammer which, in turn, fires the gun. Since the gun has to be pre-cocked, no matter what type of gun it is, the operator has to do something to cock the gun for at least the first shot.

A single-action revolver, like those in old cowboy movies, needs to have the hammer cocked by hand before each shot. The trigger press releases the hammer. There is no semi-automatic operation that cocks the hammer for the next shot.

A single-action pistol also needs to be cocked for the first shot, but since it is semi-automatic, some of the energy from the first shot is redirected to send the slide backward. This action pulls the spent cartridge case out of the chamber, ejects it, cocks the hammer and loads a new cartridge from the magazine into the chamber. Semi-automatic pistols almost always require some type of manual safety device to prevent accidental discharge between planned shots.

The usability characteristic of a single-action handgun is that the trigger press can be light and easy. Since the trigger only has to release the hammer, it doesn't take much force to operate. As a result, a single-action handgun is easy to shoot accurately because you won't move the gun as much when applying force to break the trigger.

Double-Action

As you might guess, a double-action handgun does two things when you pull the trigger: It cocks the hammer and then releases it when the trigger reaches its full length of travel. With many double-action revolvers or pistols, you can manually cock the hammer, making the trigger easier to pull since it doesn't have to cock the hammer first.

A double-action revolver's trigger may require 10 to 12 pounds of force to cock the hammer and fire a shot. As a side note, the trigger press also causes the cylinder to rotate since that operation usually happens when the hammer is cocked. Every shot from a double-action revolver will require the same trigger-press force, assuming you don't manually cock the hammer.

A double-action pistol also requires approximately 10 pounds of force to operate the trigger because it also cocks the hammer and fires the shot. While some double-action semi-automatics can only be fired in double-action, others can be selectively fired in either double- or single-action. If the pistol has an external hammer, the first shot automatically cocks the hammer, so the second and subsequent shots feel like that of a single-action pistol. So some double-action pistols actually work as hybrids between double- and single-action pistols. With these types of guns, you'll need to become accustomed to two trigger-press sensations. The first press requires more force, while the second and subsequent ones require less. Some like this feature, as the first shot requires deliberate effort, even if proficiency requires more training.

Striker-Fired Pistols

There's a third design that's common among modern polymer pistols such as Glocks, Smith & Wesson M&Ps and Springfield Armory XD-family models: striker-fired. With this design, loading the chamber by operating the slide pre-cocks a spring-powered striker (basically a firing pin) so that when you press the trigger, less force is required to finish cocking the striker and fire the shot. The first shot also pre-cocks the striker the same way, so every shot and trigger press feels the same. The net result is a trigger that operates somewhere between a single-action and double-action. Most striker-fired pistols require 5 to 7 pounds of force to operate.

HOMEWORK

It's time to go shopping! Head to a gun store so you can try pistols and revolvers with different types of operations and actions. Most gun stores will allow you to dry-fire guns so you can test them out to see how they feel. Dry-firing is simply operating the action and pressing the trigger without using ammunition.

We'll get to the safety rules shortly, but for now, even when dry-firing without ammunition, never, ever point a gun at someone! Oh, and always ask the salesperson for assistance and permission to operate any handgun. If he or she is on the ball, he or she should always confirm the unloaded status before handing you a gun from the case.

UNDERSTANDING AMMUNITION

When you walk into a big-box sporting-goods store to shop for ammunition for the very first time, you might think you just stepped into that government warehouse from the closing scene of *Indiana Jones and the Raiders of the Lost Ark*. The sheer volume and variety of ammunition boxes can be overwhelming. That's because there are lots of variables, hence lots of boxes. There are hundreds of calibers (sizes) for different rifles, handguns and shotguns. Within each caliber, there are various purposes for ammunition. Some are intended for practice, some for hunting and some for self-defense. For each of those unique combinations, there are multiple brands. The result is the plethora of colorful boxes you see on the shelves.

Let's boil the ocean a bit to make the ammunition-shopping experience a little more manageable.

CALIBERS

The first thing you need to learn is the concept of calibers. Simply put, caliber refers to size, with plenty of caveats.

Technically, caliber refers to the diameter of the bullet. A bullet fired by a .45 ACP pistol measures 0.451 inches in diameter. A bullet from a 9mm pistol measures, you guessed it, 9mm (which equals 0.355 inches) in diameter.

If you run across calibers that don't exactly match their names, don't stress too much; gun people just like to make things confusing. For example, the bullet of a .38 Special actually measures 0.357 inches. So does that of a .357 Magnum. And a .30-caliber rifle bullet usually measures 0.308 inches. Go figure.

Caliber (meaning diameter) is only part of the equation. You also need to consider the cartridge for which your gun is chambered. Different types of ammunition may use the same-caliber bullet, so you have to account for that too. One example is the .38 Special and .357 Magnum cartridges we just mentioned. The cartridge type not only defines the bullet diameter but also the shape, length and pressure that a cartridge generates. So when buying ammunition for your new gun, you're really shopping for the specific type of cartridge for which your gun is designed. It's just a matter of convenience that people refer to this as "caliber."

Be careful when shopping because many calibers sound similar in name but are incompatible, and you never want to fire the wrong type of ammunition in your gun. That can yield catastrophic results!

To illustrate the point, here are a couple of examples: If you ask for .357 ammunition, you might get either .357 Magnum, generally designed for revolvers, or .357 SIG, designed for semi-automatic pistols. Another common caliber is 9mm. While most modern 9mm pistols are designed to shoot 9mm Luger, also called 9x19mm or 9mm Parabellum, you'll also find 9x18mm and 9x23mm, which are entirely different rounds. Never fear; most modern guns have the exact type of cartridge the gun accepts stamped right on the barrel. If you're in doubt, your local gun-store staff will help you get the right stuff.

Once you narrow down the right cartridge for your gun, navigating those piles of ammo on the shelves becomes much more manageable. Next, you'll just have to choose the right ammo for your intended purpose.

PRACTICE AMMUNITION

You don't have to shoot practice ammunition through your gun when you practice, but you'll want to. Practice ammunition is designed to go bang when you shoot it, fly straight and poke holes in paper or ding a steel target. As a result, it is fairly inexpensive. The bullets themselves don't have to do anything exceptional, so the manufacturer can mold a hunk of lead into the right shape and size and wrap it in a copper jacket. For this reason, most practice ammunition is referred to as "full metal jacket."

The main reason to use different ammo for recreation and practice is cost. For example, you can find full metal jacket 9mm ammunition for $.20 or $.25 per round, especially when you buy in larger-quantity boxes of 100 or 250.

SELF-DEFENSE AMMUNITION

Self-defense ammunition isn't cheap. It will likely cost you about a dollar per round, and you should be happy to pay that. Here's why:

First, your life may literally depend on it. Part of what you're paying for is extra TLC in the manufacturing process to ensure the round will go bang when you need it to most. In all the years I've been shooting, I have yet to have a premium self-defense cartridge fail to operate. Not even once.

While reliability is important, that's not even the big deal in terms of price and function. Self-defense ammunition is carefully designed to perform within very specific parameters. In order for a handgun bullet to have maximum effectiveness, it needs to expand and penetrate to an adequate depth in the target. Remember from our earlier discussion that handgun performance is not nearly as impressive in real life as it is on television. As such, you'll want every possible advantage.

The FBI has spent decades and millions of dollars testing ammunition to figure out exactly what it needs to do to have maximum effectiveness. In short, without going into all the gory details, a hollow-point self-defense bullet should expand when it hits an organic target. There are two reasons for this: First, a larger-diameter bullet passing through the target is more likely to damage something important, thereby stopping the attack more quickly. Second, as a bullet expands, it loses energy and forward momentum. This reduces the likelihood that it will simply pass right through the target. While I can't find a documented case of a bullet passing through one person and harming an innocent bystander, it's a concern to consider.

When considering expanding bullets, you have to balance expansion with penetration. A bullet that expands to double its original diameter is worthless if it penetrates only an inch or two. That's not deep enough to get to vital organs. In fact, the FBI wants bullets to penetrate to a minimum of 12 inches in standard FBI-style ballistic ammunition testing. That may sound like a lot, but when you start to factor in things such as angle and the chance that a bullet may hit extremities first before getting to the torso, it's not overkill. So a bullet needs to penetrate, but penetration performance is contrary to expansion. The faster a bullet expands, the faster it slows down and the less it penetrates. If it expands too slowly, it penetrates too deeply and may pass through the target without doing maximum damage. It's this careful balancing act, which is different for every caliber, that makes self-defense ammo so expensive. Every bullet has to be carefully engineered to perform within a very narrow performance window.

Upgrades are available to premium self-defense ammunition. For example, many manufacturers will develop special powder blends that produce minimal muzzle flash. If you have to shoot in dark conditions, this helps minimize the risk of temporary night blindness. You also might find special coatings on the cartridge cases to aid low-light visibility and corrosion-resistance.

ALWAYS USE SELF-DEFENSE AMMUNITION IN YOUR CARRY GUN

Don't succumb to the temptation to use cheap practice stuff when you're carrying concealed. When full metal jacket ammunition hits an organic target, it's more likely to pass right through, causing far less damage than expanding self-defense ammo. Sure, it's just as lethal, but small holes mean slower times to incapacitation. Your goal is not lethality but to end the attack as quickly as possible. In fact, practice ammunition is usually more lethal to an attacker than self-defense ammo because an attacker has to be shot more times to obtain the same result. More holes mean more bleeding, but not necessarily fast enough to help your situation. If a mugger dies after he kills you, you aren't much better off, are you? It's for these reasons that almost every law enforcement agency in the country issues expanding self-defense ammunition to its officers.

HOMEWORK

If you already have a gun, you'll need to select your personal-defense ammunition. It's always important to verify that your particular gun works well with a certain brand and type of self-defense ammunition. Sometimes certain guns and certain ammo just don't get along, which may cause your gun to malfunction by failing to reliably feed a new round or eject a spent one.

When you decide on your ammo, buy a couple hundred rounds to shoot through your gun to verify that it performs reliably. You don't want to find out that your ammo doesn't work well in your gun during a fight for your life. Once you verify reliability, you can use the inexpensive stuff at the range. After you clean your gun, load the premium self-defense ammo to prepare for carry or home defense. This way, after the initial trial, you'll only need to buy a box or two of expensive self-defense ammo once a year or so.

SAFETY FIRST!

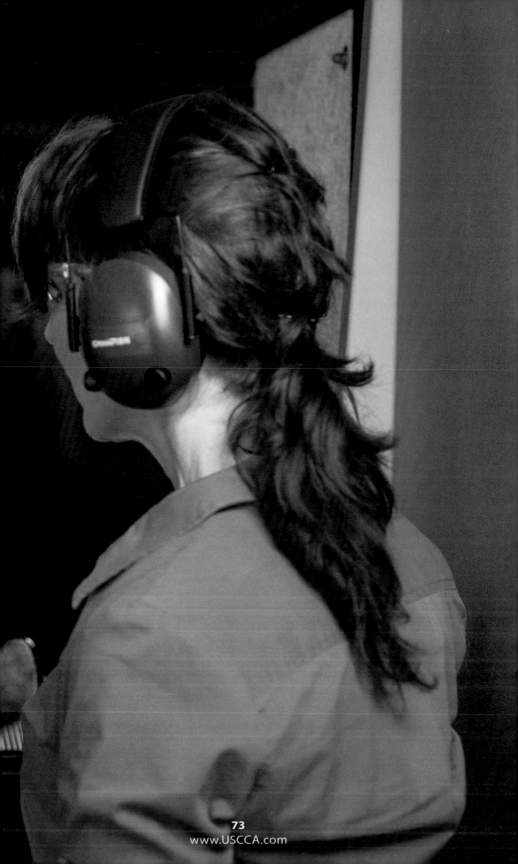

Owning and using a firearm is a huge responsibility. You hold a tool with tremendous power in your hands.

Accordingly, you need to demonstrate to those around you that you're being safe. Earlier in this series, we talked about safe ways to store a firearm at home. Now we're going to focus on how to safely handle firearms. Here you'll learn the four cardinal rules of firearms safety. Every responsible gun owner will expect you to know and follow these rules faithfully — no exceptions. In return, you should expect the same from all other gun owners and hold them accountable when necessary.

As you'll see, these safety procedures are redundant. You have to break more than one safety rule for something to go terribly wrong. Learn these rules. Make your friends and family learn them. Make sure every new shooter you take to the range understands these rules.

With that said, let's review the four rules of gun safety.

Rule No. 1: A gun is always loaded!

Do you know how many people are shot with "unloaded" guns? Too many. In fact, every time you hear about a gun accident, you can just about guarantee that the shooter thought the gun was unloaded. You might hear excuses such as:

"I thought it was unloaded."

"I didn't know it was loaded."

"I took the magazine out."

The intent of Rule No. 1 is to completely remove the "I thought it was unloaded" excuse from your vocabulary — permanently. If you never do anything with an unloaded gun that you would never do with a loaded gun, everybody is happy, and there can never be an accidental shooting.

You won't point it at someone or something that you really don't want to shoot.

You won't carelessly pull the trigger and fire the gun at an unplanned target.

You won't leave it lying around the house where someone else might pick it up and fire it.

Simply put, Rule No. 1 tops the list because it covers a lot of behavioral ground. Your attentiveness and behavior change for the better if you treat every gun as though it were loaded.

So take it seriously. Assume that a gun is loaded every single time you look at it or touch it. Pretty soon, you'll start believing that it IS actually loaded. Even when you look and verify that the gun is empty, you'll want to look again to make sure. This is a good thing. Never ignore a gut feeling to check the status of a gun just one more time to be sure. We have gut feelings for a reason.

I like to have some fun drilling this concept with new shooters. I'm not teasing them. On the contrary, I'm helping them understand the importance of Rule No. 1 in a fun and memorable way. After we review the four rules of gun safety, I pick up a gun (usually a revolver) and open the cylinder. I show the students the empty chambers and ask them if the gun is loaded. If I've done a good job teaching thus far, they'll smile and say, "Yes!"

Rule No. 2: Keep your finger off the trigger until you are ready to fire!

While I'm always reluctant to say something is absolutely impossible, the odds of a gun simply going off without a trigger press of some type are infinitesimally low.

When someone says, "It just went off," you can bet that it "just went off" because his or her finger was on the trigger.

The challenge with Rule No. 2 is that most of us naturally want to rest our trigger finger on, you guessed it, the trigger. That's why our index finger is called a "trigger finger," right? To implement Rule No. 2 faithfully, we have to practice making sure that our finger is never in the trigger guard unless we're just about to shoot. Before and after the shot, the trigger finger should be out of the trigger guard area, resting along the side of the gun. Not only does this prevent a negligent discharge of the gun, but it also clearly signals to others nearby that you are holding the gun in a safe condition.

The only way to program your brain to follow Rule No. 2 is to practice. Have your shooting companions watch you and say "trigger" any time your finger is in the trigger guard when you're not shooting. Be vigilant about this — forever. After a thousand or so safe gun-handling episodes, your brain will become programmed to subconsciously move your trigger finger at the appropriate times. This is the goal, as that's the physical behavior you will resort to under stress.

It has to become an ingrained reflex no matter what the scenario. Immediately after your last shot, does that finger come off the trigger? When changing magazines, does the finger come off the trigger? Does the finger come off between the last shot and setting the gun back down on the table or putting it back in a holster? What if you have to move during the middle of shooting? Will your finger automatically come off the trigger? What about if you are interrupted or startled while shooting? Will your brain still remember to tell your finger to back off?

If you want a fun way to build great trigger discipline, enter local competitions. Adherence to Rule No. 2 is required at all times, else you'll be disqualified. It's a great way to reinforce good habits.

Rule No. 3: Never point your gun at anything you're not willing to destroy!

Rule No. 3 means you should never, ever point your gun at anything other than your carefully chosen target. The easy part is thinking to never aim at something you don't mean to shoot. The hard part is learning to never momentarily wave the muzzle of your gun across something you don't intend to shoot. Imagine your gun has a giant lightsaber coming out of the muzzle that emits a beam two miles long. Anything that beam touches while you handle or otherwise move your gun around is instantly destroyed.

When you pick up a handgun from a shooting bench and turn to aim downrange, will it, at any time, point toward a person or thing, even for a microsecond?

When you pick up a gun to look at in a gun store, will it ever point toward the clerk or another customer while you are in the process of grasping it?

When you set a gun down on a table, is the muzzle aimed at anything you'd prefer not to shoot?

Like Rule No. 2, this one requires rigorous practice, awareness and, ideally, input from others. While at the range, never hesitate to politely remind someone to watch the muzzle.

It may sound obvious as you read this, but Rule No. 3 includes your own body and extremities, not just those of others. Consider where the muzzle points as you pick up a gun, inspect it, put it away or draw it.

Be especially cautious of muzzling your extremities, as they tend to move around and have a great probability of being in the wrong place at the wrong time.

Rule No. 4: Always be sure of your target and what's behind it!

Bullets enthusiastically go through things. That's what they're designed to do. Normal handgun projectiles will easily pass through multiple walls, wood, glass and even steel.

Understanding the persistence of a modern projectile is what Rule No. 4 is all about. Whatever you're shooting at, assume that a bullet can pass right through it. The less obvious part of Rule No. 4 is the "what's behind your target" part. Even if your target is solid and will reliably stop a bullet, you have to account for the potential of a miss. That's why indoor range facilities have expensive backstops that will either trap or safely redirect projectiles. Outdoor ranges generally have large berms of earth to catch projectiles at the back of the range area.

Rule No. 4 uses the words "be sure" for a very good reason. Unless you are absolutely positive about what's behind your target, don't shoot. Being "pretty sure" isn't good enough when it comes to gun safety. If your view is obscured, don't shoot. Be positive.

HOMEWORK

Commit these rules to memory. And then make all of your immediate family members commit them to memory. Every time you go to the range, review the rules with your partners.

From this moment forward, every time you pick up a gun for any reason, open

the action and check that the magazine is either removed or empty and that the chamber is empty. If you look at a gun in a store, and the salesperson opens the gun, verifies that it's empty and then hands it to you to inspect, open it again and verify for yourself before handling. Seriously. No serious shooter will ever laugh at you for double- and triple-checking the unloaded status of a gun. In fact, he or she will respect you for it.

Become a trigger-finger-discipline guru. When you're not actively pulling the trigger to intentionally fire a shot, make sure your finger is out of the trigger guard area and along the side of the gun. Do this until it becomes automatic. I've seen competitive shooters moving through courses who trip on a rock or board, fall flat on their faces and keep their trigger fingers out. The motion had become so second nature to them that even when falling out of control, their brains pulled their fingers away from the triggers as they were falling.

From this moment forward, visualize that giant lightsaber coming out of the muzzle of every gun you touch, destroying everything in its path. Make muzzle discipline an automatic and natural function.

Last, don't allow other shooters to exhibit unsafe behavior around you. No one wants to call out another shooter, but if he or she is unsafe, it's your duty. You can be polite. If that doesn't work, leave.

WHAT TO EXPECT AT A SHOOTING RANGE

We've talked about the four rules of gun safety, and that's an important part of what you need to know before heading to the range. The other part is range etiquette. It's always good to know how the place operates, what to expect and what others will expect of you. Here, we're going to talk about the local shooting range customs so you can not only fit right in but also be welcomed as a safe and responsible member of the shooting community.

PEOPLE WILL BE PACKING HEAT!

When you walk into a gun store or range, it's highly likely that everyone working there will be wearing a gun on his or her belt. Never fear; it's perfectly normal. After all, people who work in jewelry stores probably wear their goods too, and you'd be surprised at how many of them are also carrying a gun or at least have one behind the counter. As a business that's a potential target for crime, it's a visible deterrent. Maybe that's one of the reasons you hardly ever hear about an armed robbery at a gun store. Anyway, I only mention it because it might seem a little intimidating at first.

SAFETY GEAR

First things first. When shooting, always, always, always use proper hearing and eye protection. If you shoot at a supervised range, it'll be required, but you should want to be fanatical about this anyway. Every time you fire a gun without wearing hearing protection, you cause permanent and irreversible hearing damage to yourself. It'll take a few years to notice the effects, but every single shot causes a little more permanent deafness. As far as eye protection, remember that a chemical explosion generating up to 60,000 pounds per square inch of pressure is happening inches in front of your face. If something goes wrong and some of that hot, particle-filled gas escapes, you'll want your eyes protected. Also, you'd be amazed at how bullet fragments can bounce straight back from the target or backstop. You'll never see it coming, and if you aren't wearing safety glasses, you'll never see again. If you're just getting started and head off to a range to rent some guns to try, don't worry; the range will have extra sets of safety glasses and earmuffs for you to use. When you get going, invest in your own ear and eye protection. I highly recommend quality electronic earmuffs. These allow normal sound levels (such as conversation) to pass through so you can hear commands from the range safety officer or instructor as well as others nearby. The electronics block sound over a certain decibel level to protect your hearing. I mention this so you know it's acceptable, safe and required that everyone present wears the right safety gear.

> *"Also, you'd be amazed at how bullet fragments can bounce straight back from the target or backstop. You'll never see it coming, and if you aren't wearing safety glasses, you'll never see again."*

GUN HANDLING COMING AND GOING

If you're bringing your own gun to a shooting range, most ranges will want you to keep it in a case of some sort. The polite and safe way to enter a store or range with your gun is to have it unloaded, with the slide locked open (or, if you have a revolver, with the cylinder open and visible). In this condition, put it in a gun case. You can use the case that it originally came in if you like.

Bringing your gun in this way is the safe, polite and respectful way to do it. If you walk in the front door waving an exposed handgun, people might think they're about to be robbed! As for the unloaded status in the box, it's always best to reserve any handling of a handgun with live ammunition for the range itself or another area with a safe backstop. In general, the less you can handle a loaded gun, the better.

Be aware that different ranges have different policies, so be sure to check. If you're renting a gun from a range, don't be surprised if they insist that you buy the ammunition from them. It's their gun; for safety and liability reasons, it's perfectly normal for them to want you to use ammunition of known origin. Some ranges may ask to see or inspect your gun before you go in; that's normal too. Different ranges have different types of backstops, and certain gun-and-ammunition combinations can cause physical damage to their facilities. Also, don't be surprised if range personnel ask to inspect your ammunition if you're bringing your own. That's for the same reason.

It probably goes without saying, but unless asked, don't open your gun case until you get to your shooting lane or area. Again, that's just a good safety practice.

BE COLD TO YOUR RANGE NEIGHBORS

Being cold at the shooting range isn't rude or even anti-social. In fact, it's not cruel to be kind; it's cool to be kind … of cold.

If you shoot at a supervised range, you'll hear the range safety officer periodically hollering things such as, "The range is hot!" or, "The range is cold!" That's code for, "It's time to shoot now," and, "Stop shooting so people can change targets."

When a range goes cold, it's important to show just how cold you can be to all your range neighbors. A cold range means not touching your gun — ever, under any circumstance. In fact, some ranges have a line a few feet behind the shooting benches where everyone is expected to stand while the range is cold. That physically prevents anyone from messing with a gun. Why? When the range is cold, people go downrange to do things such as check and change targets. Never handle your gun while someone is downrange, even though your gun's unloaded. Why? Rule No. 1 — a gun is always loaded!

At an unsupervised range, you might see people handling guns while the range is cold. Ask them to please stop until the range goes hot again. A responsible shooter will thank you for reminding him or her to be safe. If he or she gives you any attitude or tells you the gun is unloaded, realize that person is a dangerous idiot. Hang on, that was kind of a harsh characterization. He or she is an irresponsible, ignorant, oxygen-wasting menace to society. And I mean that. If he or she doesn't start acting safe, pack up your gear and leave. Remember, almost everyone who was ever accidentally shot was injured or killed with an "unloaded" gun (or at least a gun the user thought was unloaded). Don't chance it, ever. If you see unsafe behavior at your range frequently, find another range.

Hey, as a bonus, since you're stepping away from the shooting bench when the range is cold, it's a great opportunity to meet your shooting neighbors.

A COUPLE OF RANGE SAFETY TIPS

Other shooters at the range will appreciate your attention to safety. Focus not only on being safe but also on demonstrating to nearby shooters that you're being safe.

Remember Rule No. 2 when at a shooting range — keep your finger off the trigger unless you're firing a shot. When looking at your target or talking to your shooting buddy, pop that finger out of the trigger area until you're ready to fire the next shot. It's safe for you and respectful to those around you. The shooters in the lanes to either side will certainly appreciate your attention to safe shooting.

Since handguns are so short, it's really easy to lose track of where their muzzles are pointed. Especially if you're shooting with others, be super careful about keeping the muzzle pointed downrange at every moment. If you turn around to say something to your shooting buddy, it's all too easy to turn the gun with your body and point it at the person to your side. Remember that big laser beam coming out of the muzzle and you'll be fine.

Also, be sure to step right up to the line when you're going to shoot. You want to avoid standing behind the line with your handgun because the muzzle of your handgun will be behind other shooters, and that will make them nervous.

IF SOMETHING GOES WRONG

Later in this book, we're going to cover some basic malfunction drills that you can do to debug a couple of common jammed-gun scenarios. If something strange happens with your gun or ammunition at the range and you're not sure what to do, just set your gun on the shooting bench, pointed downrange, and go seek the help of a staff member. Unless you're completely confident about what you're doing and can perform a fix safely, don't try to do it yourself.

HOMEWORK

Ask questions! We all hate to admit we don't know what's going on, and going to a gun store or shooting range for the first time can be intimidating. After all, it seems like everyone else there knows exactly what they're doing and you may not. That's OK. Do you know why? Gun owners are some of the friendliest people you'll ever meet, and most of them love to talk about their passion. If you aren't sure about something, just ask anyone who works there. Or always feel free to ask a nearby shooter. Far more often than not, people love to help, and most will be thankful that you asked rather than assumed.

STANCE
AND GRIP

What we're going to talk about this time may sound slightly contradictory to the earlier chapters in this book. When we talked about what a gun really does, we dove into some basic physics — mainly to point out that a bullet fired from a gun doesn't have enough momentum to knock someone off his or her feet. If it did, then the shooter would also be knocked over from that much momentum because of Newton's Third Law, which says that "every action has an equal and opposite reaction." It's pretty clear that a handgun doesn't have enough power to knock you over when you fire it, so why are proper grip and stance so important?

Here's why: Even though you won't get knocked over backward by firing your handgun, it does have recoil. The weight of the bullet and burning powder factored in with the velocity of all that stuff blowing out the fiery end means there will be some backward force against your hands and body. Not only that, the recoil will cause the muzzle to jump up and away from your target with each shot. While it's really the combination of bullet weight and velocity that determines relative recoil and muzzle flip, you can generally think of larger-caliber guns as causing more recoil.

> *"The weight of the bullet and burning powder factored in with the velocity of all that stuff blowing out the fiery end means there will be some backward force against your hands and body. Not only that, the recoil will cause the muzzle to jump up and away from your target with each shot."*

So even though your gun is not going to knock you down, you need to be able to control it and not let it control you. If you control your gun and keep the muzzle on target between shots, you'll not only hit your target more reliably but also be able to shoot faster while still impacting the target. These are the primary reasons it's so important to learn proper stance and grip.

One more thing before we get into this; you might hear a trainer recommending different variations on stance and grip as though his or her way is the only possible way to do it and any other variation will cause Jupiter to plummet into Toad Suck, Arkansas. Don't be discouraged by different opinions. If some variation works better for you, then go for it. The basic concepts apply across all variations, so don't get too hung up on details. You want to be stable so you can control the gun; everything else is details.

STANCE

Without fail, every single person I take shooting for the first time does "the Bernie." If you've ever seen that old cult flick *Weekend At Bernie's*, you might know the dance it inspired. You lean back from the waist and kind of flop around, just like dead Bernie. New shooters do the same thing. They'll step up to the line, extend their handguns, then lean way back from the hips and fire. I suppose it's a natural thing to move your head as far away as possible from the explosion that's about to happen in front of your face. It's human nature not to stick your face close to loud noise, concussion and a big ball of fire, right? But guess what? The gun can be only as far away as your arms are long, so leaning backward doesn't accomplish anything.

Here's the problem: Even though recoil isn't enough to knock you down, if you're already off balance by leaning so far back, each shot is going to throw you off a little bit more. The bottom line is that when you tilt back from the waist, the gun is entirely controlling you, not the other way around. Besides being dysfunctional, it looks kind of silly. For some reason, it's really hard to break people of this natural tendency. When I tell a new shooter to lean forward into the gun, he or she invariably thrusts his or her hips forward even farther while still leaning back with his or her shoulders.

Here's the easy way to think about a positive forward stance:

Get into a comfortable boxing stance. Your feet should be a little offset. If you're a right-handed shooter, try putting the left foot just a little forward of the right when you face the target directly. Now, here's the important part. You want to lean into the gun, but do this with your shoulders, not your hips. If you rest a nickel on your collarbone, it should be able to fall to the ground without hitting your waist. That means you're leaning forward so that your shoulders are in front of your hips, not the other way around. To visualize the right amount of lean, think in terms of the recoil holding you upright. If the gun isn't firing, you might actually fall forward. That's a slight exaggeration, but the more you lean into the shots, the better you'll control your gun.

This posture accomplishes a couple of things. First, you are using your big shoulder muscles, not just your hands and arms, to control recoil. The weight of your entire torso is also working in your favor. Second, as your shoulders roll inward and forward, that position helps prevent muzzle flip. I guess it's a musculoskeletal geometry mystery, but it works.

As far as arm positions, the easiest to learn is called the isosceles stance. That's because you put both arms forward, almost entirely extended, and they form a triangle. The gun will be positioned right in front of your face, maybe favoring the side of your dominant eye. There are other stances too (the Weaver stance, for example), and you can feel free to read up on those and experiment at your leisure. For now, the isosceles is easy to learn and probably the most natural. If your body is going to default to that anyway in a moment of stress, why not use it?

GRIP

Even though you're using large muscle groups to control the gun by implementing a good, solid stance, you'll want to pair that with a proper grip. The right grip, paired with a solid stance, will allow you to easily control almost any handgun.

If you're going to use two hands to shoot a handgun, you might as well get some benefit out of your support hand.

Rather than cupping it under the base of the grip like a teacup saucer, how about snugging it right alongside the grip so your support-hand fingers can reach around the front? You'll be amazed at how little your pistol or revolver jumps when you use a proper grip.

So how do you achieve a proper handgun grip?

Step 1: With your primary shooting hand, open your thumb and index finger. Push the web of your hand as high as it will comfortably go on the handgun grip, making sure that the barrel of the gun lines up with the bones in your forearm.

Step 2: In the accompanying photo, note how the firing hand is high on the gun and the fingers are placed high against the bottom of the trigger guard. The trigger finger is placed alongside the slide for safety.

Step 3: Wrap your fingers around the front of the grip, making sure to keep your index finger off the trigger.

Step 4: Do you see some free space on the inside grip panel of your handgun? Good, that's where the bottom part of your support hand's palm is going to go. Smack it on there, and don't worry if there's not enough room to get your whole palm on the inside grip panel. There won't be, and that's just fine.

Step 5: Now, wrap your support-hand fingers around the front of your dominant-hand fingers. Your support-hand fingers should be high (to the point of pressing against the bottom of the trigger guard).

You'll know you've got it right if both of your thumbs are somewhere near parallel to each other and touching. On Day 16,

we're going to talk about an adjustment to this grip when shooting a revolver, so just hold that thought for now.

Next time you shoot, notice how much less your muzzle jumps. Your support hand can do wonders to help control recoil when you actually put it to work! Plus, a proper handgun grip looks really cool. You'll be a hit at the range.

And those forward-facing thumbs? They naturally help you aim. Things tend to go where you point.

Getting a good, solid stance and grip is half the battle to good shooting. Once you have that down, you can focus on developing perfect trigger technique. We'll cover that in the next section.

HOMEWORK

Practice assuming a proper shooting stance in front of a mirror. As we discussed earlier, a lot of people have trouble getting a true shoulders-forward stance. If you practice the proper stance, verified by your mirror or your range buddy, it'll become second nature in no time.

Also, practice your grip so that every time you pick up your gun, you naturally perform the five steps to a solid grip in one smooth motion. The good thing is you can do this at home without firing the gun. Be sure that your gun is entirely unloaded in both the magazine and chamber before doing any practice like this at home.

THE IMPORTANCE OF THE TRIGGER PRESS

Shooting seems so easy, doesn't it? Aim the gun and pull the trigger when it's on target. How could you ever miss? Yet, as we all know, there's a lot more to it because misses happen — a lot.

Why is that? After all, we should all be able to hit a quarter from 10 yards away 100 percent of the time using almost any handgun. Rare is the modern gun that's not mechanically accurate enough to hit a target that size consistently. It's pretty easy to line up sights precisely with a target, so that's not likely the reason for misses. Modern ammunition is capable of shooting consistently enough to group into less than a couple of inches at 25 yards, so that's not the problem either.

One common complaint you hear quite frequently at the range is that the sights are off and need adjusting. But that's rarely the problem. I can count on one hand the number of times I've run across a new gun where the sights were significantly out of alignment. Usually, when someone is blaming the sights, he or she is hitting below and to one side of the target. There's a reason for those low-and-to-the-side misses, and it doesn't have to do with sight alignment.

The leading cause of a miss is an imperfect trigger press. If you think about it, the trigger press is an ideal candidate for the cause of misses. What's the very last thing that happens after sights are aligned on target? That's right, a trigger press.

Pressing a trigger is deceptively easy. There's nothing complicated about it, but it's one of the hardest handgun shooting skills to master. Notice that I've started to say "press" instead of "pull" — that's intentional. Pulling the trigger implies a rougher and more aggressive motion, such as yanking or tugging.

Here's why the whole "press" thing is such a big deal.

Earlier, when we discussed different types of handguns, we found that most handguns require a 5 to 7-pound trigger press to fire the shot. Some double-action guns require as much as 12 pounds, while some fancy single-action guns may only require 3 or 4 pounds of pressure. To be clear, your hand and finger are pushing on the handgun with 3 to 12 pounds of force every time you fire a shot.

Now, consider how much an average handgun weighs. One of the most common guns on the market, the Glock 17, weighs a little more than 2 pounds fully loaded. It so happens that a standard Glock 17 requires 5.5 pounds of pressure to break the trigger. The amount of force required to fire is twice the weight of the gun. If you weigh 150 pounds and someone exerts 300 pounds of pressure on you, who's going to move? That's right, you. The same thing happens with trigger press and a gun. When you apply 5.5 pounds of force to the Glock 17, it's going to want to move in your hand, meaning off target. Given the geometry of your moving trigger finger, guess which way it wants to move? That's right, down and to the side. If you're shooting right-handed, the muzzle will tend to pull down and to the left. If left-handed, it would tend to move down and to the right. There's the cause of "out of adjustment" sights.

The biggest key to shooting accurately is to train yourself to press the trigger without moving the gun at all. If your sights are on target and you execute a smooth trigger press without moving the gun, you simply cannot miss.

So how do you train your mind and muscles to press a trigger without moving the gun? It's a matter of practicing how to disconnect the movement of your trigger finger from the rest of your hand — because the rest of your hand is holding the gun.

Now let's talk about how to develop a perfect trigger press.

First, you have to stop what might be the major cause of jerking the trigger. If you look up "jerk" on Dictionary.com, you'll find a reference to a "spasmodic muscular movement." Spasmodic is generally not conducive to accurate shooting. Most people end up jerking the trigger to fire the shot at the exact instant when the sights are perfectly on target. However, in an effort to make a perfect shot, the results are usually not so great. When you make a sudden trigger press, you're going to move the gun. It's important to recognize that whenever you hold a handgun, the sights are going to move a little around the dead center of the target. That's natural — and OK. If you perform a good trigger press, the bullet will land somewhere in the wobble zone. As you practice more and more, that wobble zone around the bullseye will get smaller and smaller. Since you're focused on a good trigger press, your shots will all land in that ever-shrinking zone.

Second, you'll want to develop a dry-fire practice routine. Practicing without shooting live ammunition is an excellent way to develop skills because there is no distraction of a big noise and concussion every time you press the trigger. Without the noise, recoil and associated tendency to flinch, you can focus solely on perfecting technique. Your brain will remember that and repeat the same action later when the gun does go bang. The great thing is that you can do this at home anytime. Here's how you practice dry-firing.

Most modern centerfire handguns are perfectly safe to dry-fire without damage to the gun, but check your owner's manual first. Once you verify that your gun is all right to dry-fire, follow these steps to do it safely:

Step 1: Remove all ammunition from the magazine and chamber (or cylinder if using a revolver) and put it far away from your practice area. I like to line up the ammunition that was in the gun near my dry-fire target so I can see it while practicing. If shooting a semi-automatic, line up the cartridges that were in the magazine, then set the one that was in the chamber off to the side of those. It's a clear visual indicator that the ammunition that was in your handgun is no longer there. You want to be really sure your gun is empty before pulling the trigger in your home.

Step 2: Aim at a safe backstop. Use something in your room that would stop a bullet in the worst case. A bookshelf, piece of furniture or something similar is a good choice.

Step 3: Develop a sight picture on a part of your safe backstop and focus on the front sight.

Step 4: Press the trigger slowly and deliberately while trying to keep the front sight stable.

Step 5: Follow through on your shot by continuing to watch the front sight until after the hammer or striker clicks. You want the front sight to remain stable and on target before, during and after the trigger press.

Step 6: Depending on the type of handgun you're shooting, you may need to cock or reset the gun between dry-fire shots. If you shoot a double-action revolver, you can just continue to press the trigger. If you shoot a semi-automatic, you need to partially rack the slide just enough to cock the hammer or the striker.

Step 7: If you do this 50 times, you'll get far more valuable practice than shooting a whole box of ammo at the range. Next time you do shoot at the range, you'll be surprised at your improvement.

HOMEWORK

This is where your daily dry-fire practice begins. It sounds boring. It's not nearly as fun as going to the range and turning money into noise. But trust me on this. If you practice dry-firing for five to 10 minutes a day, your shooting will improve exponentially and quickly.

When at the range, practice shooting with a slow and smooth trigger press over and over and over again. Don't worry about your sights. Hold them more or less on target and focus on the perfect trigger press.

SHOOTING A SEMI-AUTOMATIC PISTOL

While basic shooting techniques such as stance and trigger control are pretty much the same whether you're shooting a semi-automatic pistol or a revolver, there are big differences in how the two types of guns operate. There is also a significant difference in proper grip, assuming you want to avoid a bloodletting in the web part of your hand between your thumb and index finger.

The big difference between shooting a revolver and pistol is how cartridges are loaded into the chamber to prepare for firing. In a semi-automatic pistol, your ammunition lives in a magazine. Inserting a magazine does not fully prepare the pistol to fire. You have to load a cartridge into the chamber first. With a pistol, you perform that operation by racking the slide.

CHAMBERING OR REMOVING A CARTRIDGE BY RACKING THE SLIDE

Racking the slide means cycling the action of a semi-automatic pistol. The backward and forward operation of the slide ejects a spent cartridge case from the chamber, picks up a new cartridge from the magazine and then loads it into the chamber. The same action can also be used to remove a loaded cartridge from the chamber in the event you need to unload your gun.

When starting with an empty pistol, you first insert a loaded magazine. Don't be gentle; smack that magazine into place vigorously. That's to make sure that the magazine catches on the internal latch and is fully seated in the correct position. One of the biggest causes of semi-automatic pistol malfunctions is an improperly seated magazine. If it's not fully engaged, it will eventually fall out the bottom of

your gun. Also, the top cartridge won't be in the right position, so it may not feed into the chamber when the slide operates.

Once the magazine is seated, you'll need to manually operate (rack) the slide. To rack the slide, assume a firm grip on the gun with your firing hand and retract the slide to its full extension with your support hand. Now, release the slide completely. Let the springs slam it forward into position; that's how they're designed to work. If you ride the slide forward with your hand to gently allow it to close, you're probably going to cause a malfunction. Don't feel the need to baby your gun; let the springs do their job.

Many handguns, especially compact ones, have significant spring force, so it may not feel easy to draw the slide all the way back. Many new shooters drift toward revolvers and thus have trouble operating a slide. Before giving up, let's discuss the right technique that will allow you to easily operate even the tightest of pistol slides. I can assure you that you are much stronger than the tightest of springs, but you have to use your big muscles, not the small ones in your thumb and index finger.

The basic idea is to use natural leverage and strength points of your body. Without instruction, most folks will hold a gun with their firing hand and pinch the back of the slide with the thumb and index finger of their support hand to pull back the slide. While the strong hand is perfectly capable of keeping the frame still against the spring pressure of the slide, those thumb and finger muscles are not exactly ideal for the job. All of the force of the spring is focused on just two fingers when you use the pinch method. You've got much larger arm

and body muscles, so why not use them? Here's how:

Step 1: First, take a firing grip with your strong hand, making sure that your finger is off the trigger.

Step 2: Bring the pistol close to your body, making sure that you turn your body as needed so the pistol is pointed safely downrange.

Step 3: Next, flatten your support hand and turn it so your palm is facing the ground.

Step 4: Extend your support-hand thumb and jab it right into your sternum. Ouch!

Step 5: Move your whole support hand over the back half of the slide of your gun.

Step 6: Close it so that your palm is on one side of the slide and fingers on the other. Now you're grasping that slide with the large muscles in the hand and arm instead of thumb and finger mini-muscles. Squeeze. Imagine you're squeezing a tennis ball. Use your whole hand, not just your fingertips.

Step 7: Keeping your support arm in the same place close to your body, push the bottom half (frame) of the gun forward like you're going to jab the target with the muzzle. By doing this, you're using your firing-arm shoulder to push the gun forward against the spring pressure.

See what we did there? Rather than pulling the slide backward, we're tricking you into pushing the whole gun forward. It's an important distinction because you're using your strongest muscles in a natural motion to do the work. It makes all the difference.

When you have pushed the gun as far forward as the slide will allow it to go, quickly release the slide with your support hand. Let the springs snap the slide closed.

Remember, don't ever try to ease the slide back gently, as the gun was designed to work properly when the springs do their job with gusto.

Just remember to orient your body so that the gun points directly downrange throughout the whole operation. This technique tends to point the gun toward your support side, so just rotate your whole body accordingly.

SLIDE LOCK AND RELEASE

Most semi-automatic pistols have a slide release or slide lock lever. Think of this as a catch that traps a small notch in the bottom of the slide. The purpose is to hold the slide open so you can perform maintenance or keep the gun in a safe condition.

On most pistols, the slide will also lock back when you fire the last round of ammunition in the magazine. When you load a new magazine, the slide will be locked in an open position. To resume firing, you can release the slide, thereby loading a new round, using two different techniques. You can depress the slide release lever. On a compact gun, this may require some force due to spring pressure. You can also pull the slide back just a hair, then release it, allowing it to close and chamber a round.

Experts disagree with each other on the right technique between these two, so practice whichever one works best for you. I always pull the slide back, but that's mainly because I'm always shooting different guns. Using the slide method, I don't have to remember where the lever is on each different pistol. If you use the same gun all the time, it's faster to use the slide release lever, and you'll know exactly where it is. It's your call, so experiment with both methods to see what works best for you.

UNLOADING A SEMI-AUTOMATIC PISTOL

While you can empty a semi-automatic pistol by racking the slide repeatedly until all cartridges have cycled into and out of the chamber, there's a safer way to do it that doesn't put so much wear and tear on your ammunition.

Always remove the magazine first; that's the source of the incoming supply of ammunition. After you cut off the supply, then you'll need to remove the round in the chamber. Since the magazine is removed, racking the slide to remove the chambered round won't insert a fresh one.

Safety first! Always rack the slide a few times after removing the magazine to make sure any cartridges that were in the chamber are ejected and gone. Tragically, too many people have "unloaded" a gun by removing the magazine only. When racking the slide a few times to clear the magazine, always look into the chamber and empty magazine well to visually verify that there is no cartridge present. If your gun has enough room to fit a finger in the chamber area, you can verify the empty status by touch too. You can't be too careful when unloading a gun.

MAGAZINE CHANGES

When a magazine runs empty or you just want to remove it to unload your pistol, you simply press the magazine release button. On the majority of modern pistols, there is a button just behind the trigger guard. On most guns, it's positioned so you can use your firing-hand thumb to depress it, which releases the magazine. A good defensive pistol will allow the magazine to drop freely out, so you shouldn't need to pull it out of the gun.

Some pistols have the magazine release on the bottom of the butt of the grip, where the magazine is inserted. Usually, these have a slide lever that holds the magazine in position. You'll also find some guns where the magazine release is a lever that's part of the trigger guard. Rocking that lever releases the magazine catch.

One last thing to consider is whether you want a gun with ambidextrous magazine releases. Almost every gun has a release on the left side, which makes it easy for a right-handed shooter to operate. If you're a lefty, be sure to choose a pistol with either a reversible magazine catch button or one already equipped with buttons on both sides.

HOMEWORK

It's time to go shooting. Most commercial gun ranges offer a selection of guns that you can rent for use on their range. For the cost of a box of ammunition and maybe a nominal rental fee, you can try before you buy. Some ranges will even credit your rental fees toward the purchase price of a new gun if you buy from them.

I would recommend trying a couple of different semi-automatic pistol models over one or more range visits. Definitely shoot a full-sized model. Remember that the larger a gun is, the easier it is to shoot and the softer the recoil. When you develop some comfort with that, you can try a mid-sized or compact model.

SHOOTING A REVOLVER

There are a few differences between semi-automatic pistols and revolvers when it comes to shooting technique and handling.

LOADING AND UNLOADING

Loading a revolver is simple and safe because the cylinder or the loading gate (depending on the type of revolver you have) is open while you do it, and the revolver is incapable of firing in this condition. It's also nice to have complete visibility of the loaded or unloaded status. With a semi-automatic pistol, you have to look into two places (the magazine and the chamber) to make sure the gun is unloaded. With a revolver, as soon as you open the action, everything is easy to see. If you see nothing but air through the chambers, it's completely unloaded. If you're at a shooting range, leaving a revolver with the cylinder or loading gate open when you're not actively shooting is a great way to show your range neighbors that the revolver is in a safe condition too.

Double-Action Revolvers

Loading a revolver is easy. Just drop the cartridges into the holes and close the cylinder. That's it. When you need to remove spent cartridge cases or live rounds, just open the cylinder, rotate the gun until the rear of the cylinder is oriented toward the ground and vigorously press the ejector rod. This drives a star-shaped extractor away from the rear of the cylinder, and that carries the cartridges with it. I only suggest holding the revolver muzzle up so gravity can help the process of removing cases or cartridges.

If you're going to use a revolver for defense, you may want to consider ways to increase the speed of your reloads. Com-

panies Safariland and HKS both make speed reloaders. These cylindrical devices are matched to your specific gun model and hold the cartridges in the exact orientation as the open chamber holes in your revolver. You insert all cartridges at once and release a lock which lets the cartridges separate from the loader and fall into the chambers. With practice, it's fast and easy to fully reload your revolver in one motion. The downside of these is that they are large to carry around in a pocket because they're about the same diameter as the cylinder. For something a little more discreet, you might consider speed strips. These rubber or flexible urethane strips hold a line of cartridges by pressure only. While you can't reload a full cylinder at once, with practice, you can place two rounds in adjacent chambers. As the rounds go into the chamber, a simple tug separates them from the speed strip.

Single-Action Revolvers

A single-action revolver, like those classic cowboy six guns, works a little differently. The cylinder is locked in place and doesn't swing out as with a double-action revolver. Single-action revolvers have a loading gate that swings open to expose one of the empty chambers. After loading a cartridge into the exposed chamber, you rotate the cylinder to move the next chamber in front of the open gate. Repeat the process until finished. Since you can only see one chamber at a time through the gate, it's important to rotate the cylinder all the way around when checking to see if the revolver is unloaded.

Unloading works one case at a time too. When a chamber is lined up with the open gate, an ejector rod will push that

single case or cartridge out of the open gate. After removing one, rotate to the next chamber and repeat the process.

If you choose to use a single-action revolver for self-defense or home defense, there aren't any great speed reloading options. You've still got to extract and load cartridges one at a time. Lots of practice will help, but it's never going to be as fast as reloading a double-action revolver.

REVOLVER GRIP

When talking about grip, we illustrated how the perfect pistol grip had both hands contacting the grip panels and both thumbs facing forward. Part of the reason for the thumbs-forward position is to keep the support-hand thumb well out of the way of the reciprocating slide. If you cross your thumb behind the slide, you might just end up with a nasty cut from the sharp bottom edge of the slide. Trust me on this one; a deep cut in the web of your hand is no fun at all.

When shooting a revolver, there's a different safety consideration. Since the cylinder has to rotate freely, there is a small gap between the front edge of the cylinder and the opening to the barrel. It's narrow, and you have to look hard to see it, but it has to be there or else the cylinder won't turn. When you fire a shot, some of the flame and super-hot burning gas escape from this gap and blow out sideways from the front edge of the cylinder. Depending on the size of your hands and the revolver in question, if you put your support-hand thumb forward, it may be in the way of this gap, and you can get burned or even flame-cut when you fire. With large-caliber revolvers, you have to be really careful about this phenomenon, as the temperatures and pressure are sky high.

So, to be extra cautious, use a slightly different grip when shooting a revolver. Just like with a pistol, place your firing hand as high as it will go on the grip. That'll help you control recoil and muzzle flip. The closer your hand is to the bore line, the less the muzzle will flip. However, with your support hand, rather than placing your thumbs forward, try crossing your thumb across the back of the revolver under the hammer. You might have to move your support hand a little farther back than on a pistol for this to be comfortable and solid.

In addition to keeping your thumb out of the way of the cylinder gap, this grip technique also allows you to use your support-hand thumb to manipulate the hammer. That's particularly helpful if you're shooting a single-action revolver that requires the hammer to be cocked before each shot. Using your support-hand thumb to cock the hammer allows your firing hand to keep the same grip without the need to shift your grip between shots.

SHOOTING SINGLE-ACTION AND DOUBLE-ACTION REVOLVERS

A single-action revolver works only one way. You have to cock the hammer manually before each shot. A double-action revolver with an external hammer offers a choice. You can cock the hammer before pulling the trigger or you can just pull the trigger to both cock the hammer and fire. If you choose to cock the hammer with your thumb, you will experience a much lighter and shorter trigger press when you fire. If you're plinking for fun or target shooting, that might be a benefit. For self-defense shooting, you always want to use the double-action mode.

A double-action revolver has no manual safety. Instead, it relies on the long and heavy trigger press that cocks the hammer and fires the shot. You really have to intend to fire a double-action revolver to make it go bang, which is a good thing when using it for defensive purposes. In a stress-filled defensive situation, you don't want to risk firing inadvertently when startled. Your hands also tend to mirror each other, so if you are fighting with your support hand, you might find the fingers on your strong hand contracting too. With a light single-action trigger, that might be enough to fire when you don't intend to. In fact, many revolver owners have a gunsmith file off the hammer spur so their guns can be fired only in double-action mode. Becoming proficient is simply a matter of practice. Fortunately, a double-action revolver is really easy to dry-fire because you don't have to reset it between trigger presses. Just keep pulling the trigger to perfect your motion.

HOMEWORK

In the previous section, the homework was to shoot a couple of models of semi-automatic pistol. Now, try a revolver or two if you haven't already. Start with a common and relatively gentle caliber such as .38 Special. Ammunition is easy to find, and recoil is modest. Remember, a larger and heavier revolver will be more comfortable to shoot. Those highly portable and lightweight revolvers are great for carry but recoil more aggressively.

DRAWING FROM A HOLSTER

If you're planning to use a handgun for self-defense, even if you never plan to carry it, you'll want to develop the knowledge and skill to draw from a holster. If you ever take a training class, you'll draw and shoot from a holster — a lot. It's one of those skills that will serve you well over the long haul, even if you choose not to carry a gun while on your daily adventures.

Later in this book, we'll get into different types of holsters. For now, focus on the basic technique. Before you get started, empty your handgun. Double-check to make sure that both the magazine well and chamber are clear, or that all cylinders are clear if you're using a revolver. It's always a good idea to put ammunition out of the room when practicing. If you get distracted during practice, make absolutely sure that the gun is clear when you resume. Check the gun again every time you pick it up; that helps with the distraction scenario as well.

To illustrate the steps, we'll talk about each component of a good (and safe) draw motion as a distinct step. As you practice and build some muscle memory, it will become one smooth, continuous motion. This is also a good time to touch on the value of practicing these motions slowly and perfectly. Don't go for speed when practicing; go for perfection. If you repeat the motion perfectly and exactly the same every time you practice in slow motion, the speed will be there when you

> *"It's always a good idea to put ammunition out of the room when practicing. If you get distracted during practice, you want to be absolutely sure that the gun is clear when you resume."*

do it without thinking. It's like that *Karate Kid* example we talked about. With all that said, here are the steps:

Step 1: Assume a firing grip while keeping your strong-side elbow in close. Focus on grasping the gun grip perfectly on the first try without the need to adjust. Be sure to grasp the grip high, right up close to the slide or hammer. Your elbow will extend backward as needed.

Step 1: This isn't a typo because this step happens in parallel with the other Step 1. As you take a firing grip with your strong hand, bring your support hand right to your sternum with your palm touching your chest. This accomplishes two things: First, it brings your support hand in close to the body to eliminate the risk of it ending up in front of the muzzle as you draw. Second, it puts your support hand in the perfect place to grasp the handgun as you bring it up into position.

Step 2: Keeping your trigger finger along the side of the gun, draw it straight up, just enough to clear the holster. Your support hand should stay right where it is on your chest for now.

Step 3: Rotate the gun to a muzzle-forward orientation so that it's pointed downrange toward your target. Think of this motion as rotating your elbow down rather than pushing the gun muzzle forward. As you rotate your elbow down, keeping it close to your body, the gun muzzle will rise until it's parallel to the

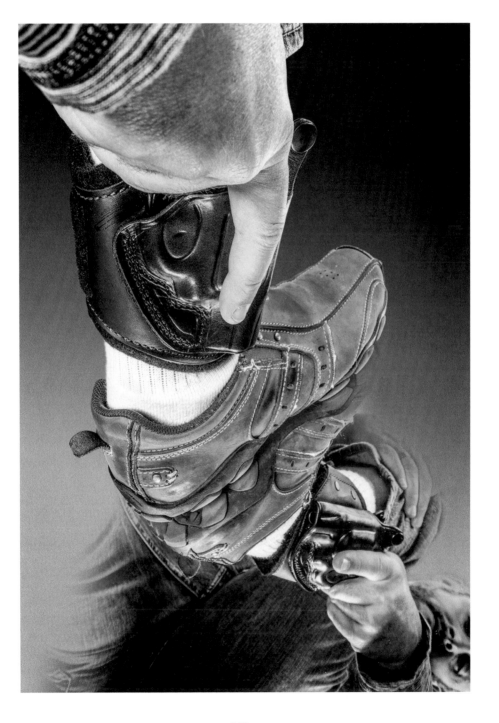

ground. When finished with Step 3, your strong hand will be close to touching your strong side, the gun will be pointed downrange, and your support hand will still be on your chest. If necessary, you can shoot from this position.

Step 4: Bring your support hand to the grip to achieve a solid two-handed hold while driving the gun forward. You want to keep the muzzle at or below the line of the target. Don't raise the muzzle above the target with this motion. Think of the front sight as rising into view to create a perfect sight picture on target.

Technically, that's a five-step process if you count the two simultaneous actions in Step 1. With the right draw motion, you can fire at any time once you rotate the muzzle toward the target.

If you have a gun with a safety, you'll need to decide when you want to disengage it during the draw stroke. Don't do it as the gun is coming out of the holster. Wait until it's already rotated toward the

target or while you're driving the gun forward. If you perform the draw correctly, your support hand will never be in front of your gun. If you want to be conservative, there's nothing wrong with disengaging the safety after the gun is fully extended. Just realize that you may not have the luxury of waiting until you get into that position to shoot.

While drawing may need to happen fast, reholstering your gun should never be a race. Take your time. Do it slowly, and look down to watch your gun go safely into the holster. The process is an exact reverse of the steps used to draw the gun. Activate the safety before you start the reholstering motion. If you shoot a double-action pistol, be sure to use the decocking lever before you reholster. Make sure that no clothing interferes with proper insertion into the holster.

It's critically important that your finger is off the trigger and out of the trigger guard during the whole reholstering motion. If your finger is on the trigger when you try to stick the gun in the holster, the edge of the holster will press against your knuckle and cause you to press the trigger and fire the gun — right into your leg.

Even as you get the hang of these steps and the motion begins to occur as one smooth action, keep practicing at slow speed. If you go for speed during practice, your motion will be sloppy. As the folks with big competitive and defensive shooting résumés say, "Slow is smooth, and smooth is fast." Try your best to do it exactly the same way every single time you practice. Your brain and body will memorize these steps, and the more consistently you can do it during practice, the better results you'll get in terms of making this an unconscious and automatic action.

The steps above describe the draw motion from an exposed belt holster. That's the best and safest way to start to develop a smooth draw stroke. When you draw from concealment, you'll need to make some modifications. Fortunately, the basic motions translate easily to those required for drawing from concealment.

If you are using an inside-the-waistband holster, you'll have some sort of covering garment, such as a shirt or jacket, to hide the gun. In this scenario, rather than placing your support hand on your chest, bring it to your belt buckle area, still touching your body, and grab a handful of shirt and lift it straight up. You'll get the clothes out of the way so your strong hand can access the gun, all the while keeping your support hand close to your body so it doesn't get in front of your muzzle.

If you choose to conceal your IWB or OWB gun with an open jacket or unbut-

toned shirt, you can use your strong hand to sweep the clothing out of the way as you reach back to grip your gun. Extend your thumb with your palm facing the ground and hook the front edge of the jacket. As you bring your hand back, fling the clothing back while reaching for the gun's grip. To aid the process of swinging the jacket out of the way, consider putting something such as car keys or loose change in the strong-side pocket. The extra weight will help the fabric swing out of the way.

HOMEWORK

The best way to develop a fast and instinctive draw is to practice frequently. Start today. Even five or 10 minutes of practice at a time a few days a week will develop your draw skills and speed at a surprising pace.

Oh, and practice dry-firing for 10 minutes!

DEALING WITH MALFUNCTIONS

Depending on the type of handgun you shoot, there are different malfunctions you may encounter and different ways to solve them. The important thing with both pistols and revolvers is to get into the habit of fixing stoppages automatically. When you're just at the range having fun, there is no real urgency to solve a malfunction. But if you put the gun down and stop your shooting, you're missing out on a great skills-development opportunity. If your gun jams while you're shooting, even if you're shooting just for fun, deal with it as though your life depended on performing the right fix. Someday, it just might. In fact, during a high-stress shooting incident, you may be more likely to have a malfunction caused by poor technique, so it's a good idea to learn to instinctively deal with problems.

It's a good idea to reduce the odds that stoppages will happen in the first place. The best way to do that is to make sure your shooting technique is solid — literally.

A semi-automatic pistol relies on some fancy physics to operate reliably. When the shot is fired, energy from the cartridge ignition and subsequent bullet launch sends the slide backward to begin the extraction, cocking and ejection process. For this to work, the frame of the gun needs to be as stationary as possible. If you allow the gun to move backward too much during recoil, the normal slide motion doesn't work properly since the frame is moving backward with the slide. The old cartridge may not be ejected, or the new one may not feed properly because the slide wasn't able to travel its full extension.

Shooters refer to this type of scenario as "limp wristing," meaning that the shooter is not bracing the gun firmly enough. I don't really care for the label, as it's not entirely descriptive.

Your wrists can be locked, but if you're not bracing your arms and body against the recoil of the gun, the odds of a malfunction increase dramatically.

The problem is compounded with smaller, lighter compact pistols. The weight of a larger gun actually helps the proper operation of the slide. With a lighter gun, more of the burden is on you to provide the stable platform to oppose recoil. The result is that many shooters complain about reliability problems with a new gun when it's really an issue of not providing enough support against recoil.

Before we get into clearing malfunctions, be sure you're providing a solid brace against recoil. That's why grip and stance are so important. If your gun is acting up, rule out shooter error first by holding on to that thing for dear life and leaning in to the shot.

> *"If your gun jams while you're shooting, even just for fun, deal with it as though your life depended on performing the right fix. Someday, it just might."*

SEMI-AUTOMATIC PISTOLS

Think of a semi-automatic pistol malfunction as a two-stage affair. If you hear a "click," or if an empty cartridge case gets hung up while ejecting, there's a simple drill that will almost always solve the problem. You'll hear shooters refer to it as the "Tap-Rack-Bang Drill," but I prefer to think of it as "Tap-Rack-Evaluate." Here's how it works.

Step 1: Keeping the gun pointed downrange, smack the bottom of the magazine to make sure it's fully seated. Improperly seated magazines cause many malfunctions.

Step 2: Rack the slide with enthusiasm. If a shell got hung up during ejection, this will clear it from the chamber area and allow a new cartridge to be inserted. If a click caused you to initiate this drill, the aggressive slide rack will eject the offending round of ammunition and load a fresh one.

Step 3: Evaluate the situation and if, appropriate, shoot.

This simple tap-rack process solves a whole lot of problems. However, some are more persistent and require additional effort. The classic example is a double-feed. This happens when the old cartridge case hasn't ejected and a new one is trying to feed. Sometimes, there are two live cartridges hung up in the chamber area. Whatever the cause, things are going to be stuck, and the tap-rack-evaluate won't fix it. It's time to move to the next level of tech support. That's still you; you're just stepping up your game.

Step 1: Using the slide lock on your pistol, lock the slide to the rear, again keeping the muzzle pointed downrange. It may take a little work to open up the slide, so use your big muscles and don't try to be gentle.

Step 2: Remove the magazine. If you do have a double-feed, the magazine is going to be stuck from the pressure of all those cartridges in a small space. Press the magazine release and yank the magazine out of the grip. At this point, you've at least prevented more cartridges from trying to feed into the action as you complete the next steps.

Step 3: Save the magazine. There's no reason to believe (yet) that there is anything wrong with the magazine or the ammo in it. If things still don't work after this drill, you can try a new magazine. Redundancy is a great reason to carry a second magazine with you at all times. Tuck the magazine you just removed under your shooting-hand arm or stuff it in a pocket. When you get the hang of this, you can work on holding the magazine between a couple of fingers while you complete the remaining steps.

Step 4: Now rack the slide several times, bordering on violently. The magazine is already out, so you don't have to worry about losing live ammo (other than what might already be jammed). The odds are that those jammed rounds are dented or misshapen, so you are inviting trouble by trying to reuse them. Get rid of them. The objective of multiple slide racks is to clear the chamber area.

Step 5: Now replace the magazine and smack it hard into place. If all has gone to plan, this is like starting with a fresh magazine and empty gun.

Step 6: Rack the slide one more time to chamber a round.

Step 7: Evaluate the situation and shoot as appropriate.

REVOLVERS

Dealing with a revolver malfunction is pretty simple. Either the cartridge fires or it doesn't.

But seriously, there aren't many mid-shooting malfunctions that you can solve with a simple drill. The most likely scenario that you can solve while shooting is hearing a "click" instead of a "bang." Hopefully, that's just an indication of a faulty round of ammunition, or maybe the hammer didn't strike the primer hard enough to cause ignition. The nifty thing about a double-action revolver is that you can just pull the trigger again. This rotates the cartridge that didn't go bang and brings a fresh one in line for another try. Even with a single-action revolver, you can just cock the hammer and accomplish the same thing. Other than that, if something fails mechanically, there's not much you're going to be able to do on the shooting line.

HOMEWORK

Your goal when it comes to handling malfunctions is to resolve them without stopping to think about it. If you own a semi-automatic pistol, you can start building malfunction-resolution habits when you practice dry-firing. Periodically pretend the dry-fire click is a malfunction and run through the Tap-Rack-Evaluate Drill. If you want to get fancy, set up some double-feeds using snap caps or dummy bullets and practice clearing that type of stoppage too.

While you're practicing some malfunction drills at home, how about working in a few minutes of dry-fire practice?

Shooting at the range can really make a difference in your automatic handling of malfunctions. Sooner or later, you'll experience a malfunction. Rather than stopping to sort things out, go immediately into your malfunction-clearance drills. Don't allow yourself to stop. Pretend that time is of the essence and that you don't have the luxury to stop shooting. The very best way to work on this is to start competing in some local steel challenge, International Defensive Pistol Association (IDPA) or U.S. Practical Shooting Association (USPSA) matches. When the clock is running, you have no choice but to deal with malfunctions on the fly.

To create practice scenarios, bring dummy rounds to the range and allow a friend to load some magazines for you, inserting a dummy or two in random order. When you're shooting and hear a click, run the Tap-Rack-Evaluate Drill and keep going. That will eject the dummy round and load the next.

HOME DEFENSE

Using a gun for home defense requires some advance planning. You want to think about things such as where and how your gun is stored, how you'll use it and where you'll be in relation to an intruder should you ever hear the proverbial "bump in the night." Let's review some things to think about so you can develop a sound home-defense gun strategy.

WHAT TYPE OF GUN?

This book is a publication of the United States Concealed Carry Association, so the natural content bias sways toward handguns. That's because it's hard to conceal a rifle or shotgun. In this section, we'll broaden the topic a little bit because a long gun can make a great home-defense gun. Let's take a quick look at various categories of guns and point out a few pros and cons. Like most things, there are no hard-and-fast, right-and-wrong answers. Different guns can be the right answer for different situations. We'll do our best to help you make an informed decision that's right for you.

Rifles

In certain scenarios, a rifle can be a great option for home defense — and not just if you live on a ranch where you might have to worry about two- or four-legged predators from a distance. By nature, most rifles are far more powerful than most handguns. They're also easier to shoot accurately because of their weight, long sight radius, two-handed operation and overall stability. Capacity can also be a big plus in the rifle category. The most common rifle in the country, the AR-15, has a standard capacity of 30 rounds (provided

you don't live in a state that places limits on such things).

Most people assume that over-penetration is a big drawback, but that's not necessarily the case. Sure, if you use a .30-06 hunting rifle for home defense, you'll have to worry about that bullet traveling through walls and into the next county. But if you consider something like an AR-15, you'll find it has less over-penetration risk than most handguns (as well as shotguns using buckshot or slugs). Standard AR-15 ammo is light and exceptionally fast. Even full metal jacket projectiles tend to upset quickly and fragment when they hit objects such as furniture and drywall. In experiments I've done shooting through multiple sheets of drywall, the AR-15 penetrates less than a standard 9mm pistol and less than a shotgun using buckshot. The speed of the projectile is actually a benefit, as it causes the bullet to self-destruct when impacting harder objects.

If you plan to use a hunting rifle (or any gun, for that matter) for home defense, think about where projectiles will go should you ever have to shoot indoors. Are there people in rooms behind your likely line of fire? For example, if bedrooms are on opposite sides of the house relative to the front door, your likely target might be between you and others.

Shotguns

It's hard to argue against the effectiveness of a shotgun. In terms of kinetic-energy figures, it's at the top of the charts. It's also at the top of the list in terms of recoil. You'll definitely know that you're shooting a shotgun.

Capacity varies with the type of shotgun. A waterfowl-hunting double-barrel can be perfectly reliable and easy to use, but you're limited to two shots before needing to reload. Many pump-action and semi-automatic shotguns can hold four or so shells in the magazine tube, so those are compelling for home defense. If you choose to invest in a shotgun made for defensive use, it's pretty easy to find one that holds seven or eight shells.

Ammunition choice is a big decision. Typical clay target or birdshot can be devastating at short range, meaning zero to 30 feet or so. Sure, it will make a big mess at distances farther than that, but the small shot rapidly loses energy and penetrating power. Larger-pellet loads such as buckshot are fantastic for defensive use, but they recoil hard, and the pellets will travel through walls like butter. Firing a single 12-gauge 00 buckshot load is like firing a .32-caliber handgun eight or nine times simultaneously at the same target. If you hit your attacker, the odds of stopping him quickly are far greater than when using a handgun.

One thing to consider is that a shotgun requires two hands to handle and operate. If you have children to corral, it might be difficult to handle a rifle or shotgun at the same time.

One last thing: Don't rely on movie cliches. While the sound of you racking your 12-gauge might scare off an attacker, always assume that you're going to have to shoot — and plan accordingly.

Handguns

The main benefits of handguns are ease of handling and portability. They're short, compact and light in comparison to long guns, so if you need to move through your house to get to kids or other family members, that's easier to do when toting a handgun. Your support hand is free for opening doors or using a hand-held flashlight if necessary.

On the con side, most handguns pale in comparison to rifles and shotguns when it comes to fight-stopping ability.

ACCESSIBILITY

We won't repeat the entire discussion here, but you have to consider the readiness of a home-defense gun. If you have kids in the house or the possibility of young ones visiting, you can't leave a loaded gun lying around, even if it's hidden. Kids will find it sooner or later. They're very curious and exceptionally talented at getting into things you don't want them to, and in this case, the results can be tragic. You'll need to invest in some type of fast-access gun safe. For more on that discussion, refer back to the earlier chapter titled "What About Children?"

LIGHTS AND LASERS

If your goal is to plan for protection against bumps in the night, remember that "night" is the key word. If you fire a gun in the dark, you need to be absolutely, positively sure what you're shooting at and what's behind it.

First and foremost, you'll want to keep a hand-held flashlight with or near your gun. If you need to move through your house or investigate something, you'll want to use a flashlight for navigation and searching. While you can mount a light on a gun, the purpose is different. A gun-mounted light is not for searching because if you're searching, you don't yet know what's there, so you don't want to point a loaded gun at unknown people or objects. We'll assume you'd much rather be pointing a flashlight should you find a family member wandering the house in the middle of the night. Weapon-mounted lights are fantastic, but their purpose is to illuminate a target, not search for one.

A laser is a great addition to a home-defense or concealed carry gun. It doesn't negate the need to properly identify your target in low-light conditions, but it does make it easier to hit a target in dark conditions. A laser won't make you shoot better and doesn't take the place of standard gun sights; it's just another tool that provides more capability. In a defensive situation, a laser allows you to shoot accurately from unconventional positions. The gun doesn't have to be held up at eye level as is normally required when using standard sights. If you're on the ground, shooting around a corner or searching with a flashlight while holding a gun in the other hand, a laser will allow you to aim. In dark and dynamic situations, it's exceptionally fast.

Where are your kids' rooms relative to yours? Given likely points of entry into your residence, will you be able to get to your kids?

What's your plan for communicating with or getting to your kids? Should you instruct your family to stay put if they ever sense something is wrong?

If you live in an apartment or shared dwelling, what's on the other side of the walls surrounding your room? How durable are those walls? Will they stop the type of ammunition you're considering using?

While these aren't the only questions you need to consider, they'll get you started. Without thinking of the details of how something is likely to happen, you might have a false sense of security about how a gun may or may not help you.

And don't forget to practice some dry-firing!

HOMEWORK

Consider how things really might happen during a burglary or home invasion.

If you were breaking into your own home, where would you enter? Does the front door, back door or a certain window offer the easiest access and best concealment?

Based on the answer to that question, where would an intruder likely be at the time you detect something is wrong? Where would you be relative to that position? Where would others in the household likely be at that time?

CHOOSING YOUR CARRY METHOD

I like to think of carry decisions as a risk-reward spectrum. While plenty of folks will offer the opinion that some ways of carrying a gun are right and others are flat-out wrong, it's more nuanced than that. If you refer back to the hypothetical scenarios in the "Dangers of a False Sense of Security" chapter, it becomes clear that potential threats are all different. Some are nearly instantaneous, seemingly appearing out of nowhere, while others may offer at least brief advance warning, assuming you pay attention to early cues.

Accordingly, when you decide to carry a gun, you'll have to balance opposing factors. You might find that things such as convenience and concealment often work opposite to quick access. For example, concealment might be excellent if you hide a gun under four layers of clothing, but it will take time, effort and maybe two hands to access your gun in an emergency situation. As a result, that concealment method might not be effective against a surprise attack, such as being mugged after turning a blind corner. On the other hand, if you're in your office and hear gunshots down the hall, you might have plenty of time to draw your gun and formulate a plan. When you think about how you're going to carry your gun, be brutally honest with yourself about your ability to access your gun in a sudden emergency while using your carry method of choice.

The other thing to be brutally honest about is your skill level at drawing a gun quickly and safely from your chosen carry holster or device. In theory, it sounds easy. Under stress, if you haven't practiced a lot, you'll likely find yourself fumbling, getting caught up in clothing or even dropping your gun. Without practice, it won't be pretty. Again, to be honest with yourself, prac-tice with the same clothing and carry con-figuration you're likely to be wearing when you're out and about. Don't practice only with an exposed OWB holster if your carry method will be IWB with a cover garment.

Let's take a brief look at some popular choices. We're going to talk about off-body and women-specific carry methods in a later chapter, so we won't address those here. The methods in this section can ap-ply to everyone.

Before we get into specific carry meth-ods, we need to talk about holster belts. Any method that relies on a belt attach-ment will require a proper holster belt — not just a thick or wide belt, but one specifically built for carrying the weight of a gun. You won't find these at your local department or clothing store. A gun belt is designed to not bend or flex, especially over time, so that it will continue to prop-erly support your gun. The best holster in the world is lousy and ineffective when paired with a less-than-adequate belt.

OUTSIDE-THE-WAISTBAND HOLSTERS (OWB)

As the name implies, this type of holster mounts to the gun belt, and the entire rig hangs outside of your pants or skirt. As the entire gun is exposed, you'll need to wear something such as a jacket or blaz-er to cover the gun — or else it won't be concealed from view. Since the gun barrel hangs down below the belt line, your cov-er garment will need to be long enough to maintain cover during motions such as bending, sitting, standing and walking.

An OWB carry solution is arguably the most accessible carry method, as the gun is exposed and easy to grasp in a firing grip. Normally, the gun will be positioned on or just behind your firing-side hip bone, so your hand is already nearby should you need to draw suddenly.

INSIDE-THE-WAISTBAND HOLSTERS (IWB)

Similar to an OWB holster in that it hangs from the belt, usually on the strong-side hip, an IWB holster is designed to allow the lower part of the holster and gun (the barrel, forward frame and trigger area) to slide inside of your pants or skirt. Only the grip of the handgun is exposed above the belt line. While this may cause a discernible bulge in the clothing under close scrutiny, most people will never notice it. Since most of the gun is behind a layer of clothing, concealment is much easier than with OWB carry. A shirt or jacket can easily cover the gun's grip, and the clothing doesn't have to be particularly long, as there is no need to cover the barrel hanging below the belt. Access is still excellent from an IWB holster, provided you practice moving your covering clothing out of the way as you draw.

You'll find different types of holsters that are designed for carry at different locations around your waist. Lots of folks these days have good success with an appendix-carry IWB holster. This is positioned forward of the hip bone on the strong side, somewhere around the 1 or 2 o'clock position. Concealment is excellent, and the draw can be exceptionally fast with practice. As with any carry method, extreme care when learning to draw and reholster is the name of the game.

POCKET HOLSTERS

While the words "pocket" and "holster" might sound redundant, they're not. Smaller revolvers and pistols are compact and light enough to be carried in a front pants or jacket pocket. The convenience factor is great because no cover garments are required, and putting a gun in your pocket couldn't be easier when you're headed out the door.

There are a few things to check when deciding to use a pocket holster. Make sure your pocket is compatible. Putting a gun and holster into a pants pocket is always easier than getting it out. Be sure that your pocket is large enough and has the right-sized opening that allows you to grasp your handgun in a proper firing grip and still remove it through the pocket opening. You don't want the combination of gun and fingers to be too big to remove from your pocket. Also, never carry anything other than your gun and holster in the same pocket. Keys, change and other common pocket items have a nasty habit of fouling up the works when you try to draw. Also, other items can get caught up in the holster and increase the odds of a negligent discharge. Accordingly, one of the drawbacks of a pocket holster is that you lose valuable pocket real estate for other daily necessities such as keys, change and a smartphone.

I've been talking about guns and holsters for a reason. Always use a pocket holster when carrying a gun in a pocket of any kind. One of the jobs of a holster is to protect the trigger from inadvertent movement, so that's why you always need one if you're planning to carry a gun in your pocket.

You'll find different types of pocket holsters. Some have sticky or rough material on the exterior while others have hook-shaped bottom sections. These features keep the holster in your pocket as you withdraw the

gun. It's kind of embarrassing to draw from a pocket only to find that the holster is still attached to the gun.

ANKLE HOLSTERS

An ankle holster seems cool and convenient, at least until you try to draw from one quickly. While concealment can be excellent, drawing from an ankle holster requires two hands and some basic gymnastics, so it's not the best solution to draw quickly while under stress. I wouldn't recommend this method for your primary concealed carry gun because of the difficulty of access. Not only do you have to pull up your support-side pants leg, but you'll also need to either raise that leg or lower yourself toward the ground to reach the gun once it's exposed. Neither of these actions is particularly smooth when trying to fight off an attacker or create distance to escape.

On the other hand, an ankle holster is a fantastic way to carry a small backup gun. Think about it: If you ever have to resort to using a backup gun, things are in a bad state already. You may be on the ground. Your attacker may have control of your primary gun. Having a spare in an unusual location just might get you out of a bind.

CLOTHING CARRY

Enterprising holster designers have come up with a myriad of ways to integrate concealed carry with clothing. Some companies, such as UnderTech UnderCover, make compression undershirts, shorts and leggings with integrated holster pockets. These are excellent for deep concealment and also make great carry methods for active folks who like to jog or ride bikes. I've also found them to be good

ways to completely hide a gun in situations where a belt holster just won't work. Just be aware that access won't be as fast as with a more exposed carry method and that you'll need to practice to make sure you can get to your gun quickly.

HOMEWORK

Today's homework is shopping — but with a condition. Your concealed carry gun is only as good as the quality of your concealed carry holster. Just as you would never fill the tank of your new Bugatti Veyron with recycled restaurant grease, you never want to tote around the gun that might save your life in a $15 budget holster. Mentally commit to spending more than $50, and maybe $100, on a quality holster. It's worth it. Kydex and leather make great holster materials, so it's a matter of personal preference as long as you buy quality. Ideally, look for a solution that will allow you to reholster your gun safely with one hand. That will make training much easier and is a great feature to have in an emergency.

Don't forget to work in 10 minutes of dry-fire practice!

CARRYING IN YOUR CAR

Whether you spend a majority of your day in the car for work or just to commute and run errands, you might need to make some adjustments to your carry habits. Both legal and physical issues need to be understood and considered if you're going to tote a gun while you drive.

LAWS REGARDING VEHICLE CARRY

Earlier we talked about how state laws differ widely when it comes to carrying a gun in a car without a concealed carry permit. Even if you do have a permit, there are some things you need to research before driving with your carry gun.

Some states require you to inform police officers during a traffic stop that you have a concealed carry permit. While laws change frequently, there are about a dozen states that have such requirements. Several states have a legal provision that requires you to inform a police officer of your carry permit or armed status if you are asked. We can't cover the nuances of every state here, so be sure to research the laws of your own state.

Your state may also have specific requirements dictating exactly how to notify a law enforcement officer that you are carrying. If it doesn't, use common sense and remember that every time an officer walks into a traffic stop, he or she is entering an unknown and potentially deadly situation. Be calm and respectful, and don't suddenly yell, "I've got a gun!" I like to simply hand over my concealed carry permit with my license. Then, the officer can initiate the discussion about whether or not I am carrying at the time. I think this casual notification removes a lot of unknowns from the situation and puts the officer at ease. In the few traffic stops I've had through the years, never has the fact that I'm carrying a gun been

an issue. The fact that I have a permit seems to have given the officer the confidence that I'm not one of the people he or she has to worry about, and not once has the officer ever asked me to surrender my gun during the stop. Some officers will request to hold on to your gun until the stop is over. If that's the case, think about how you can do this while keeping the gun in its holster. Be sure to communicate clearly with the officer to understand how he or she wants you to handle the situation.

Also check if your state has any unusual restrictions on how you can carry a concealed gun in a car. Some states will want that gun attached to your person, whether you're in a car or not. Accordingly, it may not be legal to keep your gun in a console or glove box, even if you have a concealed carry permit. You can thank politicians for the confusion.

One last note about carrying in a car: Do not store your gun in the same location as your registration and insurance card. It's not a good idea to open the glove box when asked for your registration during a traffic stop only to expose a handgun to the police officer. Save yourself and the officer some unnecessary stress and always keep your papers somewhere your gun is not.

CARRY POSITION AND ACCESS

Carrying while seated in a car presents some challenges, the least of which is the issue of comfort. If you carry on the belt, either IWB or OWB, you might find that your deep-seated position in a car causes your gun and holster to dig into your side. That's not fun. What's worse is that you may not be able to easily access your belt-carried gun. If you're a right-handed shooter and are driving, the seat belt latch is going to be right where your gun is located. Combine that with your very bent body position and you'll find that it's far tougher to draw than when standing or even sitting in a more upright position.

If you don't spend a lot of time in a car, you might just choose to live with these inconveniences in order to benefit from the right carry method for the rest of your day. However, if you make your living in a car or truck and spend hours per day driving, you might want to consider a carry method that is optimized for a car.

Cross-Draw Holsters

A cross-draw holster mounts on your support side rather than under your shooting hand. Rather than angling the grip of the gun slightly forward or vertically like most standard IWB or OWB strong-side holsters, a cross-draw holster has an aggressively negative cant when worn in the traditional position. Because it's on the opposite side of your body and you have to reach across your belly area, it's easier to grasp the gun when positioned this way.

If you're a right-handed shooter and are in the driver's seat, the seat belt doesn't interfere nearly as much as with a strong-side holster, so it's easier to reach your gun from the seated position in a car. It's also a lot more comfortable, as you can mount the cross-draw holster a little more forward of where you would typically put a strong-side belt holster.

The drawbacks of a cross-draw holster become apparent when you're using one while you're not seated. When standing, you have to be very careful not to sweep the muzzle of your gun across others or even your support arm as you draw the gun across the body. It's very easy to point the muzzle at anything or anyone on your support side when drawing. For this reason, many ranges and training instructors will not allow you to use a cross-draw holster at their facilities or in their classes.

Shoulder Holsters

Another carry method that can be great for career drivers is the shoulder holster. If you remember the old cop show *Miami Vice*, that's the basic design that Don Johnson used when he played detective Sonny Crockett.

When standing, a shoulder holster has similar disadvantages to a cross-draw holster. Your gun is oriented straight behind you, so technically, it can be pointed at anyone back there. As you draw, you run the risk of sweeping the muzzle across your support arm and anyone to your side.

However, in a car, the placement up high on your torso on the support side keeps your gun completely out of the way of a seat belt and your folded midsection area. A shoulder holster is exceptionally comfortable for long drives, and it's easy to access your gun from it.

Ankle Holsters

While an ankle holster isn't the best solution for primary carry when up and about, it makes a pretty good car-carry solution. Think about it: You're already bent nearly in half from sitting in a car seat, so it doesn't take much to reach your gun.

Next time you're seated in a car, touch your weak-side ankle to see exactly how much effort it will take to reach a gun. Additionally, when you're seated, your pants leg typically starts to ride up, so less effort (if any) is required to move your pants to access your gun.

WHEN YOU HAVE TO LEAVE YOUR GUN IN THE CAR

First of all, never leave your gun in a car overnight. While it's tempting to have a gun live in your car, it's up to you as a responsible citizen to do everything you can to keep your gun out of the hands of thieves. Far too many guns are stolen from cars parked overnight in the owners' driveways or apartment parking lots. Don't provide the temptation.

With that said, there are times that you might need to leave your carry gun in the car for short periods. Common examples include picking up kids from the inside of their school or going to the post office. For some unknown reason, concealed carry is prohibited at all United States Post Office facilities. If you are frequently in and out of your car and face a long list of places where you have to temporarily remove your carry gun, you might want to consider a car lock-box solution. Small handgun lock boxes from GunVault come with cables that

can semi-permanently attach the lock box to your car. If you want to get really fancy, you can check out the Console Vault. That replaces the center console of your vehicle with a more permanent interior gun safe.

HOMEWORK

Do a little thinking about the balance of your days. If car travel is normal and occasional for you, I wouldn't recommend switching to a car-optimized carry method. If you spend the majority of your daily time in a vehicle, check out alternate holster solutions, such as cross-draw and shoulder rigs. If you go this route, realize that you'll need to be extra careful about your draw motions. It will always be your sole responsibility to be able to draw without exposing yourself or others to unnecessary risk.

You guessed it. Today's homework assignment is 10 minutes of dry-fire practice.

CARRYING AT WORK

If you're considering carrying at work, you'll first need to investigate legal and policy issues. Only then can you begin to evaluate potential carry methods.

LEGAL ISSUES

Because the government likes to get involved in everything, there might be legal issues that relate to your ability to either carry at work or keep a gun in your car while you're at work. Believe it or not, on rare occasions, government meddling can actually work in your favor. Clearly, if you work for an organization that falls under the long list of places where concealed carry is prohibited, you might be stopped in your tracks right there. For example, if you're a teacher, the odds are good that you can't carry at your place of work — though even that is starting to change in some places. You might run into similar roadblocks if you work for almost any state or federal government agency.

Outside of that, again, depending on your state, you may run afoul of weird carry laws that prohibit carry in places such as churches, restaurants, sporting venues, day care centers, medical facilities and even businesses located in buildings that are partly occupied by government entities. For example, there was a case a while back about an office building that had one office leased to a United States senator. Concealed carry was prohibited in that entire building. Cases like that bring up a spiderweb of constantly changing regulations, some of which have inspired laws that actually protect the rights of lawfully armed citizens. For example, many states now prohibit employers from prohibiting the storage of guns in cars parked in company lots. That's a lot of prohibiting, isn't it? These laws make sense. If you choose to carry a gun for self-defense but can't even have it in your car when at work, you don't really have a right to carry at all, do you? To stay within the bounds of corporate policy and the law, one would have to go to work and then rush home to collect his or her gun before continuing his or her daily travels.

Because of all the potential legal landmines, it's important that you carefully evaluate the environment where you work and investigate state laws that may affect your ability to carry. If you work in a leased space that's part of a larger property, and some tenant spaces are leased to prohibited types of entities, you might be at risk. Always check carefully before you move on to the next step.

POLICIES

Policies are where things get interesting, and you get to make decisions with huge consequences. How's that for pressure? Legal prohibitions are pretty clear. You know where you can lawfully carry and where you can't. If you choose to violate those laws, you're going to face some potentially serious consequences.

When it comes to carrying at work, even if the law doesn't have anything to say about it, your employer might. Some companies, especially larger ones, may overtly address the concealed carry issue by stating a policy in the company handbook. With rare exception, the default policy will be that concealed carry is not permitted at work. Smaller companies often don't have policies like this documented in a formal employee handbook, so the question is most likely not addressed at

all. There are employers that do allow or even encourage concealed carry, but that seems to be the exception.

When faced with a policy that prohibits concealed carry, you have to make a decision. Violating that policy is almost certainly grounds for instant termination. We're certainly not going to advocate that strategy, as that is a personal decision. On the other hand, many law-abiding citizens are tired of feel-good policies that create gun-free zones, making those areas perfect targets for disgruntled former employees, armed robberies or even acts of terror.

Depending on which study you review, as few as two mass shooting events have taken place outside of gun-free zones since 1950. Put simply, from a statistical perspective, nearly every single mass shooting event in the past 65 years has occurred where someone created a policy prohibiting concealed carry. Again, we're not advocating that you ignore your employer's policy. It's their company and their property, and they get to make the rules. You'll have to weigh the risks of something bad happening at your place of employment when you are disarmed by policy against the risks of getting caught violating the rules and losing your job. If you choose to ignore corporate policy and carry anyway, you certainly won't be the first person to do so — or the last.

> *"From a statistical perspective, nearly every single mass shooting event in the past 65 years has occurred where someone has created a policy of no concealed carry allowed."*

If your employer has no specific position on the matter, you have a different decision to make. You can either ask in advance or beg forgiveness later. I'm not an attorney, so this is in no way, shape or form qualified legal advice, but I might be inclined to follow the "ask forgiveness later" approach. It's likely that if you waltz into your boss's office one day and ask if you can carry a gun to work, the answer will be a resounding, "No!" On the other hand, if there is no policy against it, you might have a fighting chance to plead your case should anyone ever find out that you carry concealed. After all, you have a state-issued permit, and the employer has not barred the practice on their property. But winning the technical argument may be irrelevant, as you still might lose your job.

So there's your list of fairly rotten choices. Disarm yourself and hope for the best when you're on company time — or take a chance at violating the rules by exercising your right to defend yourself and risk losing your job. That's a call only you can make.

CARRY STRATEGIES

Unless you work in a business that embraces carry, you'll probably want to use a deep-concealment method if you choose to carry at work. Additionally, you'll want to make sure that your carry strategy provides plenty of gun security. You may get fired should anyone ever spot your gun, so you need to be absolutely sure that your gun can't fall out or become exposed throughout the range of your normal work activities.

Whatever you do, don't choose an off-body carry method such as a purse, pack or briefcase. In a work environment, that pack or purse will be set down and left unattended at times. You simply can't afford the risk of being separated from your carry gun. Have you ever gone to lunch or a meeting while leaving your briefcase or pack behind? Or even left it at the office inadvertently? I have.

You might want to consider an under-clothing carry option for work. When I worked for companies where carry wasn't prohibited (but I'm fairly certain it would have been frowned upon), I used a compression-shirt holster from UnderTech UnderCover. These shirts fit tightly — like athletic compression shirts — but they have elastic holster pockets sewn in under each arm. Many have Velcro straps that secure a gun into the holster pouch. You'll find a variety of styles and colors for men and women, so take a look.

The benefit of undershirt and under-shorts carry is that they don't depend on specific cover garments. In my environment, I had to wear business casual with tucked-in button-down shirts. A sports coat to cover an IWB holster would have been out of place, plus there was no way I was going to be able to wear the jacket every minute of every day. Additionally, the odds of seeing a gun peeking out sooner or later were near certain. For these reasons, I went to the compression-shirt holster. You can tuck in a shirt or blouse without interference from the holster. The

gun, being located under your arm, is invisible — even if you carry a medium- or full-sized model.

The downside is access. Unless you equip all your work clothes with false snap buttons, you're going to have to yank out your shirt or blouse and reach under it to get to your gun. The time required to draw and fire your gun may be double that of a belt-carry method.

Compression shorts or belly bands offer similar benefits. The shorts and belly band allow you to carry in a more traditional waist location, and you can tuck in a shirt with no telltale tuckable holster clips. You still have to tear away the tucked-in shirt, but at least you don't have to reach underneath and across your body to access your handgun.

Some people have great success with solutions such as SmartCarry. This pouch wraps around your waist and is completely covered by a pair of pants. The gun holster pouch rides down low in front of your groin area. Carried with the right pants, the gun is invisible. Besides, people at the office won't be staring at your crotch.

HOMEWORK

Do your homework on applicable laws. Discreetly check for any existing (and documented) company policy on concealed carry. Based on what you find, you may have a big decision to make.

Also, do 10 minutes of dry-fire practice!

CARRYING TIPS FOR WOMEN

Many newer women shooters who make the decision to carry concealed default to purse carry. I absolutely understand why. We guys have one basic dress code: pants and shirts. Technically, the pants and shirts are not attached. This allows us to carry a gun in the waist area fairly easily. Even if the shirt needs to be tucked in, it's not too hard to find an effective holster that can reside underneath. It's not always convenient for guys to carry on the belt, but it's almost always possible.

Women don't have that luxury. Sometimes, women do wear pants and shirts or blouses as separates. However, many women's pants (not to mention that whole fashion thing) are unable to hold a big bulky gun belt that's required to support a belt-carried gun and holster. While skirts offer the theoretical possibility of waist carry, the belt or support system challenge remains. The real fly in the ointment appears when dresses enter the daily wardrobe. With no separation between the top and bottom halves, the only waist-carry option would be an Old West-style exterior gun belt slung low around the hips. Of course, we know that won't work either.

For all these reasons (and probably some I've neglected to mention), women have a much tougher time figuring out how to carry concealed than men. So I get the need to consider purse carry. Nonetheless, many carry with traditional methods. The Well Armed Woman, a retail and training organization, did a survey recently to find out how most women actually carry a gun, and the results may surprise you.

Among the women surveyed, a whopping 50 percent carry on the waist using traditional IWB (40 percent) or OWB (10 percent) holsters. That really surprised me. Apparently, these women have made a conscious decision to significantly alter their wardrobe choices in order to carry a concealed gun. Another 13 percent carry in the waist area with a belly band. Approximately 15 percent carry higher on the torso with a bra holster (8 percent) or shoulder holster (7 percent). Seven percent use an alternative carry location such as a deep concealment pouch, ankle holster or thigh holster. What about purse carry? Only 13 percent. While the survey respondents are probably more likely to be serious concealed carriers, the numbers are still surprising.

The numbers support women's naturally protected zones on the body. Carrie Lightfoot, CEO and Founder of The Well Armed Woman, explains, "Women have a few 'sweet spots,' and the challenge for most of us is to identify our own and use them to our advantage. Carrying anywhere in the 'prime zone,' which includes the circumference of our bodies from our hip bones to our underarms, is what we strive for."

Let's look at a few carry methods that work for many women, along with some pros and cons to each.

PURSES

Many women default to purse carry not only for convenience but also due to lack of knowledge about alternate on-body carry methods. A purse is ever-present for many women and the only place they can carry other daily necessities such as wallets, phones and car keys. As a result, it's a natural choice for concealed carry. It's easy and requires no special wardrobe

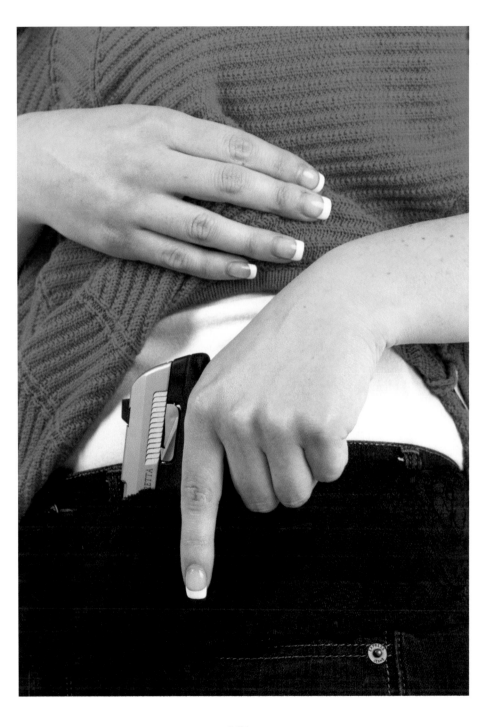

planning. The gun is also in the same location regardless of the clothing choice on any given day.

Purse carry encounters significant drawbacks. The biggest is that your gun isn't attached to your body. Purses get set down and may be out of direct reach for periods of time throughout the day. Since a purse isn't always in your direct possession, others (such as children) can get into it and access your gun without your immediate knowledge. A purse is also a theft target. Losing money to a purse snatcher or attacker is bad enough, but losing your only means of self-defense can be fatal.

If you choose to go this route after carefully considering the drawbacks, be sure to use either a purse with a dedicated holster pocket or an insert system that creates a dedicated gun-carry area. A dedicated gun pocket not only protects you from things getting hung up in the trigger and creating a negligent discharge but also keeps your gun instantly accessible and oriented for a smooth draw.

CLOTHING CARRY OPTIONS

UnderTech UnderCover and other companies with similar products offer a variety of compression-clothing carry options. Various shirts allow carry of a gun and spare magazines in secured gun pouches under each arm. Compression shorts have sturdy gun pockets that allow carrying behind the hipbone without the need for a traditional belt and holster. Recently, UnderTech UnderCover released Concealed Carry Leggings. With gun pouches front and back, a woman can discreetly carry in the appendix position or behind the hip

bone. To all casual observers, the woman is just wearing normal leggings.

The benefit of clothing carry options like these is that they do not rely on gun belts and bulky holsters. You'll have much more wardrobe flexibility. Better yet, they keep your gun secure against your body. UnderTech UnderCover owner Tammy Magill points out other reasons to carry on the body: "Purse carry can be a good option, but it weighs you down. When you wear a gun on your body, you don't feel that weight. And with a purse, you have to worry about where it is all the time."

Just be aware that some of these carry options can come at the cost of slower access to your gun. The deeper your gun is buried, the better it's concealed but the harder it is to access. There's a good way to overcome this obstacle: Practice, practice, practice!

BELLY BANDS AND CORSETS

Belly bands wrap around the body, have built-in gun holster pockets and operate independently of other support gear (such as belts). Since they require no special gear and can be placed higher or lower on the body, they're exceptionally flexible with different wardrobe choices. Some people use one like a traditional but self-supporting belt holster and carry a gun in a normal hip position. They're also quite good at setting up a cross-draw configuration by which you store your gun on the support side. Most belly bands have multiple pockets cut at different angles so you can choose your best fit and gun location. You can also flip the belly band inside out, which orients the pockets differently and gives you more choices.

For a more feminine take on the belly band, check out the Carry Corset from Dene Adams. Founder Anna Taylor has four small children and tried all the classic women's carry methods but was unsatisfied with gun security. After at least seven carry-method attempts, she decided to invent her own system. Reminiscent of the structure of a belly band, the Carry Corset leverages some of the biological differences between men and women. As Taylor explains, "Women are built to carry weight in this area, so even carrying the weight of a heavy gun in this position is easy. The weight of the gun doesn't bother me one bit. Also, as women, we're naturally protective of that area, so we're constantly aware of the gun." While there is decorative lace on the outside to aid concealment, this is a solid piece of gear. The best part is that it's a great way for a woman to carry a gun on her body.

BRA HOLSTERS

Flashbang Holsters has created an industry out of non-traditional carry methods for women. With a line of holsters invented by women, they're well-tested and offer useful solutions for complex wardrobe situations. The classic Flashbang Holster mounts on the center of a bra and holds a gun with a Kydex clamshell holster that keeps it in place and protects the trigger. Reaching under a shirt or blouse, you take a normal firing grip and pull the entire gun straight down to release it from the clamshell. As the gun is located in the chest area, concealment is outstanding, and women can wear tight clothing without telltale printing. Another design mounts to the side of a bra, inside the cup. This is a great option when wearing scoop-neck tops because access to the gun is from above — through the neckline.

Enterprising women are constantly inventing new ways for women to carry, so keep your eyes open. Just be aware that less-conventional carry methods require you to practice and train in order to carry and draw safely.

HOMEWORK

Before defaulting to purse carry, think carefully about minor wardrobe adjustments that might allow you to carry on your body. If you have no choice but off-body carry, I get it. Just remember that carrying a gun is supposed to be comforting, not comfortable. We're talking about a lifestyle change that may save your life. It's not always going to be easy, and you're going to have to make some adjustments to your daily routine to carry every day in a safe, responsible manner.

Don't forget to work in 10 minutes of dry-fire practice! While you're at it, if you've already chosen a daily carry method, do 20 draws from your holster using a carefully unloaded gun. If you can work in draw practice every time you dry-fire, you'll be developing mad skills in no time.

SELF-DEFENSE IS NOT LIKE THE RANGE

At the beginning of this book, we talked about the dangers of a false sense of security. While that chapter focused on the fact that merely having a gun present may not help you in a self-defense encounter, there's a lot more to it. In this chapter, we're going to raise a lot of questions. We are going to make you think about your current level of self-defense preparedness and give you a baseline from which you can decide on future training. A false sense of security can get you killed, so think through these issues and be honest about your current level of readiness.

Using a gun for self-defense is nothing like using a gun on the shooting range. By way of analogy: Just because you scored uber-platinum expert level on the iPad version of GT Racing doesn't mean you can take on Jeff Gordon at Talladega. You've got to not only get in a real race car, but also spend a few decades on the track experiencing the pressure, track conditions and head-to-head competition with a few hundred other drivers.

Let's look at some of the differences you're likely to encounter in a self-defense situation.

STRESS FACTORS

First and foremost, if you're forced to use a gun to protect yourself or loved ones, you're going to have to deal with the most basic of human physiological responses. Your lowest-level brain functions are going to go into fight-or-flight mode. In conjunction with a massive adrenaline dump, your body and brain are going to start doing weird things.

Tunnel Vision

Many (and probably most) violent-encounter survivors report experiencing tunnel vision. When the brain detects a threat, it naturally focuses on that actual threat more than the surrounding environment. Other things going on in the vicinity aren't deemed relevant to your immediate survival. When your earliest ancestor was about to be trampled by an irritable woolly mammoth, I doubt he or she stopped to notice that the turnip crop was coming in early that year.

At first, this seems like a healthy thing. Why not allow yourself to focus on your threat? The biggest reason to train beyond this instinct is that criminals don't always attack solo.

Consider the case of Joseph Robert Wilcox: While shopping in a Las Vegas-area Walmart, he encountered Jerad Miller. Miller (and, as we'll soon see, his cohort Amanda Miller) had just executed two Las Vegas police officers at a nearby CiCi's Pizza. When Jerad Miller entered the store and fired a shot into the ceiling, Wilcox decided to put a stop to things. However, as he approached Jerad Miller from behind with his own concealed carry gun, he was shot and killed by Amanda Miller. While we don't know exactly what Wilcox saw, it's likely that his brain fixated on what he perceived as the threat: Jerad Miller. It's doubtful that he ever saw Amanda, and that cost him his life.

More and more frequently, criminals work in teams. If you see someone holding up a cash register, there's a decent chance that some other "shopper" inside the store, or perhaps a "bystander" outside the store, is providing lookout and backup duty. If you choose to or need to get involved to protect yourself, you'll need to force your brain out of its natural programming and look around for other potential threats.

Auditory Exclusion

Another potential response you might expect is auditory exclusion. Auditory exclusion is similar to tunnel vision in that the brain filters out information deemed not critical to immediate survival. Many who fire their guns in a life-or-death encounter report not hearing the shots at all. Certainly, the noise is there, and the mechanical parts in your ears detect it. It's just that your brain chooses to shut off that incoming loud noise signal. As a result, you don't hear the shots.

Perhaps this is part of the reason why people have trouble recounting how many shots they fired or how many were fired at them.

Tachypsychia

If you think brain behavior is weird with tunnel vision and auditory exclusion, how about when it alters your perception of time? You might experience a slowing down of events. Experts call this phenomenon "tachypsychia," and people who have experienced it report that they felt like everything was moving underwater — slowly and deliberately. Certainly, things are happening in real time, but in survival mode, your brain might move into hyperdrive and present the perception that everything is moving in slow motion.

The point of noting all these interesting physical phenomena is to illustrate that calm and peaceful plinking on the range doesn't prepare you for an armed encounter. Knowing and expecting these things is the first step, and that alone can help you better deal with things such as post-incident interviews.

While there's not much you can do to prevent physiological responses, knowledge of these potential handicaps may help you minimize their effects. For example, training to purposefully look in other directions around your focal point may help you remember to scan the immediate environment if you see one suspicious individual.

MOVEMENT AND MORE MOVEMENT

If you read internet forums, you'll likely run across cyberspace ninjas espousing ridiculous strategies such as training for head shots in case attackers are wearing body armor. That's fine if you and your adversary are both stationary. Now assume that your attacker is running and moving erratically while trying to kill you. Then consider the fact that you are also running and fighting. Now that defender and attacker are both moving full-speed in mortal combat, how's that head shot strategy working out?

I'm poking fun at internet commandos, but the point to remember is that in a self-defense encounter, you won't be shooting at a stationary target who's just waiting to get shot. Your target will be doing his or her very best not to get shot by you. This is why it's so important to take face-to-face training classes with certified instructors. They'll teach you about shooting, moving and how to escape.

WHO'S THE BAD GUY?

Here's another thing to contemplate from the safety of your home: How sure are you that you'll be able to differentiate the bad guys from the good guys in the swirl of a chaotic encounter?

If someone threatens you with violence, that's a pretty easy call since you know you're a good guy or girl. What if a bystander also draws a gun? Is that your attacker's backup, an armed citizen deciding to help you out or perhaps an undercover law enforcement officer?

What if you're walking down a dark street and you see a man striking a woman? Will you come to her aid? What if he's an undercover cop and the woman just attacked him with a knife? Or maybe she's an undercover cop who got surprised by some thug she was in the process of arresting. Or maybe it's an abusive husband or boyfriend, and that woman needs help right then and there.

What if you just shot an attacker in self-defense? What if a guy wearing jeans and a T-shirt points a pistol at you and shouts for you to drop your gun? Is it an off-duty cop or your attacker's angry brother-in-law?

These examples illustrate the fact that the actors in a self-defense encounter may not have easily identifiable roles. You might know who's on your side and who's not, but then again, that may be difficult to discern in a split second. No amount of target shooting is going to prepare you to deal with this.

HOMEWORK

Your homework is to research live training classes that focus on self-defense. Finding a qualified instructor will be easy; just go to the USCCA's training page and look for certified instructors in your area. If you can't find one there, check your local gun stores to see who they recommend, then carefully review the instructor's feedback online. Pay particular attention to feedback from students who have attended other training programs elsewhere. If someone has only been to one class, how can he or she compare the relative quality of instruction?

This is not going to be easy or cheap. You'll likely spend a fair amount of money for your first class. That's OK. Remember, it's literally a matter of life and death.

VIRTUAL TRAINING

W atching reruns of that '60s sitcom *The Flying Nun* won't make you a 787 Dreamliner pilot any more than a movie marathon of *The Bourne Identity* flicks will make you a self-defense gunfighting ninja spy. However, you can learn a lot of information through books, photos and videos. The key is to make sure the content is vetted and not just the ramblings of some random internet warrior.

Keep in mind that virtual learning is great as an educational supplement, but nothing takes the place of hands-on training when it comes to learning new mental and physical skills. As long as you recognize that you may experience a false sense of security by relying too heavily on virtual learning — knock yourself out. We can't all attend monthly instructor-led classes and hit the range for practice every few days. Besides, there are plenty of non-physical topics we need to learn and review, such as tactics, the law and case studies.

Let's discuss a few ways to help you develop your overall knowledge level, along with respective pros and cons of each.

WEBSITES

Start studying and digesting quality education and training information today. Better yet, do it for free:

USCCA Education: www.USConcealedCarry.com/Education/

The USCCA produces hundreds of free articles online, available to anyone. Visit the website and explore topics such as Self-Defense & Home Defense or True Stories. You can also subscribe to a free newsletter to get notifications of new articles.

USCCA Free Downloads:
www.USConcealedCarry.com/Free-Downloads/

Even without USCCA membership, you can download free reports such as *23 Proven Strategies for Self-Defense* and *6 Things You Didn't Know Would Happen*

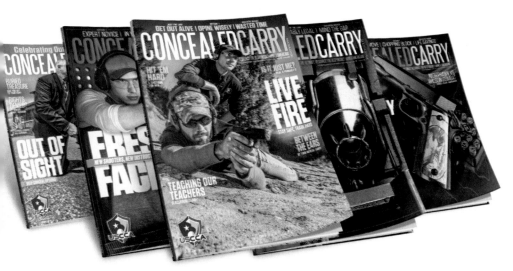

When the Police Arrive. When you join the USCCA, you'll have access to much more.

MAGAZINES

Concealed Carry Magazine: www.ConcealedCarryMagazine.com

There are plenty of gun magazines on the racks, and most of them have good content about guns and gear. However, only one magazine focuses exclusively on content and articles that will help you defend yourself and your family. *Concealed Carry Magazine* has gun and gear reviews too, but it's focused on those products that relate to concealed carry. I like reading a story about the Winchester 1873 lever-action rifle as well as the next guy, but if I want to learn tactics and strategies that will help protect my family, I go here.

BOOKS

USCCA Store: www.USConcealed-Carry.com/Store.asp

If you're the type who prefers to learn by turning pages, there's a mountain of books available on self-defense and concealed carry. If you want a simple place to start, where titles are reviewed and hand-selected for their training value, check out the USCCA online store. You'll find plenty of diverse titles to keep yourself busy.

VIDEOS

If you're looking to move beyond the printed word and still photos, you can find a wide array of online video and DVD content produced by reputable trainers. Here are a couple of sources to get you started:

USCCA Store: www.USConcealed-Carry.com/Store.asp

The last time I looked, there were nearly 20 different DVD training sets available. Topics range from choosing the right firearm to gun laws to self-defense for women — and everything in between. Check out the *Armed & Ready: Your Comprehensive Blueprint to Con-*

cealed *Carry Confidence* program. This set contains eight DVDs covering topics such as "Dangers We Face," "Deadly Force Decisions," "Get On Target" and "Gear Up," just to name a few. The training kit also includes a companion guide and a booklet titled *10 Drills to Improve Your Shooting*. It's a great one-stop set that'll get you off and running in the right direction.

After you finish that program, consider the three-DVD set *Advanced Gunfighting & Survival Tactics*. There, you'll learn more advanced self-defense concepts such as how to maintain control of a firearm during a violent encounter.

The National Shooting Sports Foundation: www.YouTube.com/User/TheNSSF/Featured

The National Shooting Sports Foundation engages and promotes the shooting-sports industry and is funded primarily by manufacturers. It produces high-quality educational videos covering a wide variety of topics ranging from politics to basic shooting skills and defensive tips. The best thing is that the videos are vetted and produced by experts. You'll be getting reputable information and content.

INTERNET FORUMS

There can be great value in sharing ideas and knowledge with people just like you. One of the good things about the internet is that it facilitates immediate discussion with a whole world of folks who share your interests and concerns. You can log on to a forum with a question or comment and get instant access to an unlimited number of opinions from others.

However, there's a downside to forum life. You don't know who's on the other end. It's entirely up to you to figure out if the person on the other end of the string knows what he or she is talking about. Over time, you can start to discern who's credible and who's not based on the nature of his or her comments. If you're new to all of this, that's a risky proposition since you may not know enough to determine what is valid information and what is not. Sadly, people can get in serious trouble following unverified advice they picked up online.

If you want to have lively discussions with others, that's fine. Internet forums can be great for that purpose. But until you develop your own advanced levels of expertise, be very careful about putting into practice things you read online.

There's a wealth of information to be gleaned online and in the stores; digest it at your leisure. Just be sure that the source is reputable before you invest time and effort into learning new skills and tactics. Also remember that reading about something or watching a video is no substitute for live training and physical practice.

Reading will certainly increase your overall knowledge, but it won't hardwire physical and mental responses to sudden and unexpected events. Practice and repetition do that.

Depending on which expert you listen to, it takes somewhere between 2,000 and 10,000 repetitions of a new skill for it to become an automatic response. That's the reason so many of the homework sections throughout this series call for basic skill practice such as drawing from a holster and dry-firing.

> *"Reading will certainly increase your overall knowledge, but it won't hardwire physical and mental responses to sudden and unexpected events. Practice and repetition do that."*

HOMEWORK

Once again, it's time to go shopping! Pick out the medium of your choice (book, video, magazine or online content) and invest in some quality virtual training material. You can't always practice at the range, so find good sources of information to read when you have some downtime.

And don't forget to do a few dozen holster draws (with an unloaded gun) and dry-fire practice. If you can work those two things into your schedule just a couple of times per week, you'll be far ahead of the vast majority of fellow gun owners.

LIVE TRAINING

NO
SHOOTING
THIS SIDE

RANGE OFFICER

I t's important to understand the difference between training and practice. Both are important, but practice without training won't get you very far.

Training is intended to teach you new skills. An instructor, who presumably already knows these skills, demonstrates techniques and shares knowledge. Once you have acquired that knowledge, you can then begin to practice your new skills until you perfect them. It's important to note that training isn't a one-time thing. Another valuable function of a professional trainer is to monitor your execution and provide feedback and correction. If you learn a new skill but are doing it wrong, it's important to spot that before you make your incorrect technique permanent through practice.

When it comes to developing the knowledge and skills for self-defense, there's simply no substitute for live training. This program is intended to get you started on your journey, but in no way will it teach you everything you need to know. While a virtual education like this can pass along knowledge and certain skills, it can't provide the critical function of monitoring and feedback.

If you decide to get a concealed carry permit, your state will probably require you to take a concealed carry class. In almost all cases, these classes don't qualify as self-defense training. Concealed carry classes are intended to teach you the basics of the laws of your state and maybe some basic gun-handling tactics. Unless your instructor goes well above and beyond the required material, you're not getting defensive training. If your state class does not have you out on a live range learning and practicing techniques such as shooting

and moving, issuing verbal commands and performing malfunction drills, you need to consider yourself still at step zero after completing that class.

So, run — don't walk — to get yourself scheduled for a real training class.

WHAT TO EXPECT

Your instructor (or the school's website) should tell you exactly what will happen during the class. It will probably be a combination of classroom and range work, so plan for both environments — dictated by local weather conditions. Most ranges tend to be out in the boonies by necessity, so don't count on too many comforting amenities; plan for a day mostly in the field.

Every instructor is different and has his or her own style. Just remember that you are paying your instructor to make you better, and that may require him or her to be direct and honest with you. As an example, during a class I attended years ago, I thought I was hot stuff knocking the center out of my target. My instructor came over and started teasing and taunting me (all in good fun) while having me do a shoot and reload drill. With all the distraction from him, I started to fumble and mess up royally. It was a great lesson that showed me how quickly my perceived skills could degrade under just a tiny bit of induced stress. We had a great laugh after he explained what he was trying to teach. Go to class with an open mind, and welcome correction. You're paying for teaching and correction, not meaningless affirmation. If an instructor tells you how wonderful you are when you're not, he or she is putting your life at risk down the road.

With all that said, there's nothing wrong with seeking out an instructor who is personable and who has good communication skills. There are lots of people out there with "Train Here" shingles on their doors, but a far smaller number of them know how to teach. Teaching is an entirely different skill set, so do your best to find someone who knows his or her stuff and how to effectively communicate that knowledge to others.

WHAT YOU NEED

Unless otherwise instructed, plan to bring the following:

• Shooting glasses. You'll want to protect your eyes.

• Hearing protection. Ideally, get a set of electronic earmuffs. These will protect you against hearing loss but still allow you to hear instruction and range commands while shooting.

• A hat with a brim. You don't want flying brass to land in your glasses, so always wear a hat while at the range.

• A shirt with a tight collar. You definitely don't want hot brass going down your shirt while you're holding a loaded gun. It burns; trust me. Proper clothing not only protects against burns but also prevents the wearer from waving around a loaded gun while trying to stop the burning.

• Your gun. If you have more than one, bring a backup in case your primary one breaks. It would be tragic to waste your class tuition over a broken gun.

"Unless your instructor says otherwise, bring an OWB holster. Be sure to use one with a reinforced mouth that allows you to safely reholster using just one hand."

• A good holster and proper gun belt. Unless your instructor says otherwise, bring an OWB holster. Be sure to use one with a reinforced mouth that allows you to safely reholster using just one hand. Also, make sure it's a standard strong-side (firing-hand-side) holster. Instructors won't want you using a nontraditional holster such as a shoulder, ankle or cross-draw model. You'll be shooting in a line with other students, so your holster must facilitate a drawing motion that doesn't allow the muzzle of your gun to point at anyone else.

• Ammunition. Your class should provide information on what type and how much you need.

• A water bottle or cooler full of water bottles (if your class is out in the boonies). You might be outside for most of the day, so you want to stay hydrated and sharp.

• Notebook and pens or pencils. Even if you prefer to take notes with a computer, a notebook is better suited for the range.

• Things to make your time outdoors more pleasant, such as sunscreen and bug spray.

FOLLOWING UP AFTER TRAINING

In your class, you will learn (but not perfect) new techniques. Repeated practice after the fact is where you start to claim expertise in those newly learned skills. Practice, practice, practice!

Take thorough notes so that when you get home, you can practice what you learned the right way. Don't go for speed. Practice slowly and deliberately — not only for safety but also to program the right movements into your brain. If you repeat a technique the exact same way over and over in practice, the speed will come on its own because your actions will be smooth and repeatable.

Sometimes, if you go to multiple training classes, you might find that equally reputable instructors contradict each other. That's fine, and nothing to be overly concerned about. Each of us has our own preferred way of doing things, and rarely is there only one correct shooting technique. When faced with this situation, I like to try the new way on the range enough times to give it a fair shake. After hundreds of repetitions over one or more range visits, I'll decide which method works better for me — the new one or the one I knew before. Hey, Jimi Hendrix played the guitar behind his head, and I suppose he managed to do all right with it.

HOW TO FIND GOOD TRAINING

The first step is to find an instructor. Check out the USCCA Certified Instructor database at USCCAInstructors.com/ InstructorList.asp. You'll see both certified and associate instructors. USCCA-certified instructors have successfully completed a three-day instructor course from the USCCA. Associate instructors have valid training credentials from other nationally recognized training organizations and can use USCCA materials.

If no trainer is listed for your local area, check local gun stores for recommendations. Most maintain a relationship with one or more training organizations.

However you find your class, be sure to check the feedback from previous attendees. As review sites such as Yelp have limited information on shooting schools, you might have to dig to find the information you need. Ask around.

Ask local gun-store employees. If you know anyone in local law enforcement, ask what he or she has heard. In short, do as much homework as you can. It's not just the tuition at stake, but also the quality of information you'll learn. It literally can be a life-or-death decision.

If there is nothing satisfactory in your area, plan a training vacation! There are plenty of outstanding national shooting schools, including (but certainly not limited to) Gunsite, Thunder Ranch, Rangemaster, Shootrite Firearms Academy and the SIG Sauer Academy. You can't go wrong at any of those, but you'll likely have to sign up early and wait for a slot.

COMPETITION

Many cranky gun people poo-poo the idea of firearms competition as a way to train for self-defense. You'll hear things such as, "Competition will get you killed on the street." I think they're missing the point. Competition is not self-defense, nor is it any kind of self-defense simulator. Even IDPA (in which competitors navigate "real-world" scenarios such as homes, restaurants and banks while seeking and shooting cardboard bad guys) is not a real-world simulation.

Competition improves your self-defense skills by giving you lots of practice at the basics: aiming, quickly picking up an accurate sight picture, transitioning from one target to the next, shooting and moving, accurate rapid fire, and, perhaps most importantly, operating your gun under stress. When your gun goes click instead of bang during a competition, the clock keeps running, and spectators keep watching. It's up to you to figure out how to get your gun back

in action as quickly and safely as possible. That's great practice for basic shooting and administrative skills. Besides, it's a heck of a lot more fun to develop skills like that by competing on a Saturday morning than by standing around your house, practicing drills over and over.

Just to be clear, cardboard targets don't shoot back, and the stress of competition in no way compares to that of fighting for your life. Use competition as the training aid that it is — a fun way to get better at operating your gun. Add tactical self-defense training to that and you'll be good to go.

HOMEWORK

Find a class to attend. It'll hurt, as none are cheap, and the class will cut into your free time. Trust me on this one: Once you take a quality training class, the light bulb will go on, and you'll realize how much you don't know.

Don't forget to get in some holster draws and dry-fire practice.

PRACTICING AT HOME

One of the best things you can do to improve your shooting does not involve actual shooting. Why? Without the flash, bang and concussion to distract you, it's much easier to focus on the fundamentals of shooting. Also, when you're at a live range, it's oh-so-easy to get distracted by the temptation to shoot things rather than perform boring routines designed to improve your technique.

What's really nifty is that the brain and muscle habits you develop in the quiet environment of your home will translate to skills at the live range. Things such as trigger-finger press become permanent muscle skills when you add the flash and bang back into the equation. It's just like that *Karate Kid* analogy we talked about earlier. Practice the "wax on, wax off" when you're not fighting in the dojo and you'll be amazed at the muscle memory that seemingly appears out of nowhere when you need it most.

Let's look at some ideas for how you can improve your defensive handgun skills from the comfort of your own home.

DRY-FIRE PRACTICE

We've talked about this throughout the series, but I'm going to re-emphasize it here. Why? There's nothing you can do that will make a more dramatic improvement in your shooting skills — period.

"The biggest reason for missing a target with a handgun is a poorly executed trigger press. All of the other required elements you need to hit a target are either non-factors or are easy to perform."

That's a pretty bold statement, but it's true. The biggest reason for missing a target with a handgun is a poorly executed trigger press. All of the other required elements you need to hit a target are either non-factors or are easy to perform.

Any modern handgun is more than accurate enough to hit the intended target every single time in a defensive encounter. Any modern self-defense ammunition is accurate and reliable enough to hit the target every single time. Lining up your sights with your target is not hard to do. Either the sights are on target or they aren't. There's no question about it. Misses almost always happen after the sights are on target and you begin the motion of firing your gun.

To review, dry-firing is easy, but you must be exceptionally careful with your procedures each and every time you practice. Remember, you're pressing the trigger on a real handgun, so it is imperative that you still follow the four safety rules:

1. Treat your gun as though it were loaded.

2. Don't put your finger on the trigger until you are ready to (dry-)fire.

3. Never point your gun at anything you're not willing to destroy.

4. Be sure of your target and what's behind it.

When dry-fire practicing, you still need to choose a safe backstop that is capable of stopping a bullet. That's an extra layer of insurance in the event that a live round makes it into your dry-fire routine.

The steps are straightforward, but be sure to follow them faithfully every time:

Step 1: Remove all ammunition from the magazine and chamber (or cylinder if using a revolver) and put it far away from your practice area. I like to line up the ammunition that was in the gun near my dry-fire target so I can see it while practicing. If shooting a semi-automatic, line up the cartridges that were in the magazine, then set the one that was in the chamber off to the side of those. It's a clear visual indicator that the ammunition that was in your handgun is no longer there. You want to be really sure your gun is empty before pulling the trigger in your home.

Step 2: Aim at a safe backstop. Use something in your room that would stop a bullet in the worst case. A bookshelf, piece of furniture or something similar is a good choice.

Step 3: Develop a sight picture on a part of your safe backstop, and focus on the front sight.

Step 4: Press the trigger slowly and deliberately while keeping the front sight stable.

Step 5: Follow through on your shot by continuing to watch the front sight until after the hammer or striker clicks. You want the front sight to remain stable and on target before, during and after the trigger press.

Step 6: Depending on the type of handgun you're shooting, you may need to cock or reset the gun between dry-fire shots. If you shoot a double-action revolver, you can just continue to press the trigger. If you shoot a semi-automatic, you may need to partially rack the slide just enough to cock the hammer or the striker.

DRAWING FROM A HOLSTER

Earlier, we talked about the detailed process for drawing safely from a holster, so we won't repeat that here. Instead, we'll focus on the importance of practicing your draw stroke.

Your home is the perfect place to practice drawing from a concealed carry position. You'll do this following all safe dry-fire procedures, so you'll be using an unloaded gun. You're still going to treat it as though it were loaded, right? Your home provides more flexibility than you may have at your local range. Many indoor shooting facilities don't allow drawing from a holster because of the way the lanes are set up with shooting platforms in front of each station. No worries; you can do everything you need to in the privacy of your home. Besides, you can take your time and not worry about nearby folks watching you experiment with various types of draws from concealment.

When you do practice at home, after you have double-checked that your gun is unloaded and made sure there is no ammunition anywhere nearby, dress as you would when you carry in public. If you use an IWB holster with a shirt to conceal your gun, practice that way with your shirt in place. You'll want to replicate the exact scenario you would be working with should you ever have to draw your gun in self-defense.

RELOADS

While you're dry-fire practicing, you can also work on magazine changes or revolver reloads.

If you use a semi-automatic pistol, when you hear the click of your dry-fire trigger press, release the magazine and insert a new empty one. Like any other physical skill, this one requires practice and repetition. If you don't work on that, you'll fumble should you ever have to do it for real.

By practicing with empty magazines on a regular basis, you'll work out kinks and find ways to optimize your process. You'll figure out how and where to best store a spare magazine for easy access. You'll learn how to store it so that the bullets are oriented properly in the forward insertion. In short, you'll find your own habits that make reloads as error-free as possible.

If you have a revolver and use a speed reloader, you can buy snap-caps or inert training rounds to practice unloading empty cases and reloading fresh cartridges. Never use real ammo for reloading practice.

USING HAND-HELD LIGHTS

A weapon-mounted light is great for illuminating a target just before you shoot, but you don't want to use that for searching. If you hear a bump in the night, you don't want to end up pointing a gun at a relative or visitor.

Using a separate light is a skill that requires practice and debugging. It sounds easy on paper, but until you try to use a gun with a light in the other hand, you're not ready to go with that plan. Imagine trying to change magazines while holding a gun in one hand and a light in your other. See what I mean? You can do it, but it requires practice. Similarly, how are you going to handle your phone to call for help? The more you can practice these scenarios, the better you'll perform if you ever have to use those skills under stress.

HOMEWORK

Establish a weekly routine for home practice. Try to make room in your schedule to allow for uninterrupted practice for just 15 minutes at least twice a week. During this time, practice dry-firing, drawing from concealment and changing magazines.

Also, you might feel silly doing it, but walk through your house a couple of times at night with an unloaded gun and a hand-held flashlight. Don't just think about what a break-in scenario would look like; walk through it. Imagine hearing a door or window break, then start from that point. Would you instinctively go to your kids? If so, walk the steps to find flaws in your home-defense plan. If no one else is living in your home, think about where you could and would take shelter while calling for help. Do you have concealment or cover available in that place? It's important to put yourself in that scenario by walking the steps. That's the only way you'll find the pros and cons of the plan that should already be forming in your head.

SIMPLE RANGE DRILLS

If you go to the range to just plink and have a little recreational fun, you'll improve your shooting over time. Hey, I'm the first one to admit that half the times I go to the range, it's just to have a good time, and I'm not doing any focused drills or structured practice. Shooting is an enjoyable pastime, after all! But if you want to make big progress, you'll want to practice with a purpose. Fortunately, that can be fun too.

Let's take a look at some ways you can improve the value of your range time with a variety of methods ranging from cheap and easy to more complex and expensive.

TIMED HITS ON TARGET

Once you start to get comfortable with your handgun and are making measurable progress with basic accuracy and trigger control, you can add time into the equation. Shooting for time helps with two basic skills: getting your sights on target for the first shot, and recovering from recoil and getting back on target for the next shot. Timed shooting also adds just a little bit of stress to your practice routine. You might be surprised at how many little errors a small amount of induced stress can reveal.

I'm partial to a routine called the "45 Drill" because it requires no special targets or equipment, and you can do it at almost any range — indoor or outdoor. Just bring paper plates to the range and staple one on your target. Ideally, the "45 Drill" target is supposed to be 5 inches in diameter, but who's counting if the plate is a little bigger? Now, put it 5 yards downrange. Your goal is to get five shots on the paper plate in five seconds. Get it? That's four fives, hence the "45 Drill" name. If your range al-

lows you to draw from a holster, draw and shoot in the five seconds. If not, just start from a low-ready position, with your gun pointed downrange at a 45-degree angle toward the ground.

There are infinite (plus 17) different drills that shooters have developed to improve their skills, so feel free to explore others.

ALTERNATE YOUR HANDS

The ideal way to shoot a handgun is using both hands as described earlier in this series, but you may not always have that luxury. If you are carrying a flashlight or using a cellphone, you might have only one hand available for your gun. Be sure to practice shooting with your strong-side hand only and support hand only every time you go to the range.

MULTIPLE TARGETS

One of the core skills that most people don't practice as much as they should is target transitions. Aiming at a single target and firing multiple shots is a great way to practice basic accuracy and skills such as trigger control. If you want to improve the core skills that will help you with defensive shooting, it's also a good idea to practice getting on a new target and quickly firing a shot.

Even if you shoot at an indoor range that allows only one primary target per shooting position, you can work on target transitions. On your piece of cardboard backing, tape multiple smaller targets or mark different areas on a large target. Rather than trying to shoot all bullets into the same bullseye, fire at one, transition to the next and then go back. You're not moving the gun a lot, but at least you're practicing acquiring a new sight picture before pressing the trigger again.

SHOOTING STEEL

If you have access to private property or an outdoor range at a club, you might have the option to shoot steel targets. Unlike hitting paper targets, you'll know right away if you've succeeded because of the noise. Let's be clear: Steel targets can be a great training aid, but they won't help you learn specific defensive shooting skills. They will help you develop basic marksmanship techniques, such as shooting fast and accurately, getting a quick first hit on target, transitioning between multiple targets and getting repeated hits on a target.

Don't just go shooting anything made of steel; you have to use the right stuff. Steel that's too soft, too close or inappropriate for the ammunition you're using can be dangerous. In fact, using the wrong steel or ammo can cause bullets and fragments to bounce right back at you, causing serious injury to you or others. That is yet another reason to always wear safety glasses anytime you fire a gun. Stick to steel targets made for shooting, and follow manufacturer recommendations on caliber, bullet type and minimum distances carefully.

Plates and Plate Racks

If you have access to a club with an outdoor range, the odds are good that they'll have a plate rack. These have five or more steel targets lined up in a row. When you hit one of those targets solidly, it falls down out of view. After you hit all targets on the rack, a tug on a rope leading back to the shooting line resets the whole rack. No, attackers aren't going to line up like this in the real world, but shooting steel plates is a great way to improve your ability to transition between multiple targets quickly. It also helps you learn how to shoot fast without jerking the trigger. Last, it makes you think about each and every shot. You should be able to knock down each plate with only one shot. Most plates are 6 or 8 inches in diameter, so you'll have to be accurate. The best part? It's really fun! You can improve your base skills while having a great time.

You also might find either round or square individual free-standing steel plates. They come in all sizes and mount to two-by-four boards standing upright. The nice thing about these is that you can place them wherever you like. Put some at short range, others off to the side and others far away. They don't move, but again, it's a great way to develop speed and target-transition skills.

> *"There are infinite (plus 17) different drills that shooters have developed to improve their skills, so feel free to explore others."*

Texas Stars

You also might encounter a steel target called a Texas Star. This looks a little bit like a windmill with a steel plate at the end of each vane. When you hit one steel plate, the star goes off balance and starts to turn and rock. As you hit others, it may rock even faster. Now you're shooting at not only multiple targets but also multiple moving targets. Again, it's just a fun way to improve your core marksmanship and target-transition skills.

ROTATING TARGETS

Most indoor ranges have target hangers that allow you to set your target at varying distances using a pulley system. Some newer ranges have turning target capability. These systems allow you to program the target hanger to rotate 90 degrees at random intervals. Normally, you see only the edge of the cardboard target backing. The system will rotate the target so that it faces you for a set amount of time, maybe two to five seconds. It's up to you to see the target, aim and fire before it flips back to the hidden position. It's a great training aid.

Recently, I had the opportunity to try out a new invention: the Pivotal Trainer from Triumph Systems. This is a portable flipping target stand that you can take to an outdoor range. The target has a no-shoot silhouette on one side and a bad guy silhouette on the other. The system randomly presents one or the other to you, and you must decide whether or not to shoot and act accordingly before the target rotates back out of view. Set up multiple for a real challenge.

SHOT TIMERS

If you want to make real improvements with your training, you need ways to measure your progress. Sure, targets are part of it because you'll see your accuracy improvements on paper. But another important improvement metric is time. How fast can you draw and get on target? How long does it take you to fire multiple aimed shots? Fortunately, the answers to these questions are easy to come by.

A shot timer is a nifty little electronic device that operates on the sound of gunshots. Once the clock starts running, it captures the time elapsed every time it hears a shot.

For example, you can set it to offer a starting beep randomly. When you hear the beep, draw and fire whatever routine you want to track. When finished, the shot timer will show you the number of seconds between the starting beep and the last shot. It also will tell you about any shots in between.

Shot timers are also a great tool to use at home when practicing dry-firing. Most can be used in a "par time" mode that measures a predetermined amount of time from the start to the end of the drill. For example, you might set it up to offer a random starting beep and then give you three seconds to draw and do three dry-fire shots before the end-of-drill beep.

Once you invest in a shot timer, you'll think of a million ways to use it.

HOMEWORK

Next time you go to the range, practice at least 20 shots throughout the session using your support-side hand only. If you're anything like me, it'll feel awkward, but it's a skill we all need to develop.

Also, while you're there, try out the "45 Drill" or any other that catches your eye. Be sure to record your score and time so you can track your progress.

Now, when you practice dry-firing, be sure to do some repetitions with your support hand only. Most people tend to flinch when shooting with their off-hands, and dry-fire practice is the best way to overcome that.

AFTER DAY 30

We've reached the end of *30 Days to Concealed Carry Confidence*. The rest is up to you. We've introduced some of the legal and skill concepts that you'll need to continue to learn, but consider this just that — an introduction. If you've completed all 30 days of this program, congratulations! That's a great start. Now it's time to concentrate on improving the basic skills you've learned so far. It's also time to consider advance legal planning. Just as you would acquire hazard insurance to protect your home against fire or natural disaster, you can also make preparations in advance for the legal aftermath of a self-defense incident.

ONGOING SKILL DEVELOPMENT

Self-defense skills, whether shooting skills or tactics skills such as awareness and planning, are perishable. We must use them in order to stay sharp. Throughout the program, we've talked about the importance of skill development, virtual training, live training and practicing at home. If you decide to carry a gun for self-defense, all of these activities must continue. The professionals don't practice skills until they get them right; they continue to practice until they can't get them wrong.

Earlier, when we talked about some of the benefits of virtual training through books, videos and online articles, we said they are valuable for learning certain types of things but are no substitute for live training. Moving forward, you can derive another benefit of virtual training. Staying abreast of the latest strategies, techniques and tactics will give you inspiration and ideas that you can put to work in your own skill-development regimen. Subscribe to *Concealed Carry Magazine* or at least the USCCA's email list.

Continue to watch videos. In short, try to learn something new every day.

LEGAL PLANNING

Earlier in the series, we talked about natural, instinctive physiological responses that might work against you in an armed encounter. One of the big risks is that these normal, human responses may hurt you in the legal aftermath of a self-defense shooting. Natural responses such as auditory exclusion, tunnel vision, stress, fear and a dozen other things will probably make you a terrible witness because you probably don't (yet) know exactly what happened. Many (or even most) survivors of shooting incidents can't accurately recall how many shots they fired and, when asked, they usually underestimate. Even experienced shooters may remember firing a couple of times, only to find that they emptied a 15-round magazine during the encounter. Counting the number of shots is just not something your brain deems essential to survival, so that information is often stored away or not recorded at all.

The natural confusion and filtering out of important factual information can actually harm you during the subsequent investigation and legal process. While you had to process every detail of a life-threatening encounter in a split second, others will be evaluating every detail from the comfort of office chairs and unlimited time. It's not fair, but it is what it is.

To protect yourself legally, you need to develop a layered strategy in advance. First, think long and hard about how and when you converse with responding officers about the incident. Yes, you always want to be cooperative. After all, you're the victim, and you were just defending your life. On the other hand, the sooner you try to share details, the more likely you are to say things that just aren't accurate. In the heat of the moment, most people will talk way too much — well before their brains have had time to settle down and process what happened. Consider the "number of shots" question as just one tiny example. If the responding officer asks you how many times you fired, you might answer to the best of your recollection and say, "Two or three." However, as we've just shown, the real answer may be far greater than that because your brain excluded information that seemed extraneous at the time. How's that going to sound in the courtroom later? "Ladies and gentlemen, this citizen vigilante claimed he only shot the deceased twice, yet hard, factual evidence shows he fired his gun 12 times."

To protect yourself from yourself and your good intentions, tell responding officers that your intent is to cooperate fully. Tell them you were attacked. Tell them you'll press charges. In other words, tell them the most basic facts that establish you were acting in a defensive capacity. Then, ask for time to process. "Look, I will fully cooperate and give you all the information you need, but I need a little time to process what just happened." This type of approach should not be foreign to responding officers. When a police officer is involved in a shooting, investigators realize that the officer involved needs to have time to decompress from the stress of the event, and the interview often takes place well after the situation has calmed down.

The first step is to think, plan and develop a strategy for how you will handle the post-incident interrogation. Yes, your natural instinct will be to blab in an effort to be helpful, but somewhere in your brain will be that plan you considered in advance.

In addition to mental preparation for a worst-case scenario, you should also consider lining up legal assistance now — before you might need it. Consider finding a lawyer who is well-versed on legal self-defense principles. Find one who is comfortable in an offensive role rather than as a defense attorney. After all, you're not guilty, and you have to mount an affirmative defense, not a passive one. It's an entirely different legal approach. After finding a good candidate, you can schedule an initial consultation to become a client, so to speak. Now, if you ever need to make that phone call, you at least have a starting relationship with a lawyer who can help you. You don't want to be shopping for self-defense attorneys from a jail cell.

Better yet, consider joining a self-defense legal protection network. Earlier in the series, we talked about the USCCA Self-Defense SHIELD program. Consider connecting with the USCCA for more information on this important legal and financial protection.

Now that Day 30 is complete, the rest is up to you. I hope that we've helped you get off to a great start on your never-ending journey to assume responsibility for your own protection and that of your family. Remember, the best strategy is always avoidance, but when that's not an option, you are your own first responder. The more seriously you approach your continuing journey, the better the odds that you'll prevail if ever caught in a life-threatening situation.

Best to you and yours, and shoot safe!

NOTES